Dec 18
10c
7/13/17
U= 6

Days Like These

Days Like These

*Even in the Darkest Moments,
Light Can Shine Through*

Kristian Anderson
with **Rachel Anderson**

ZONDERVAN.com/
AUTHORTRACKER
follow your favorite authors

ZONDERVAN

Days Like These

Copyright © 2012 by Rachel Anderson

This title is also available as a Zondervan ebook. Visit www.zondervan.com/ebooks.

This title is also available in a Zondervan audio edition. Visit www.zondervan.fm.

Requests for information should be addressed to:

Zondervan, *Grand Rapids, Michigan 49530*

Library of Congress Cataloging-in-Publication Data

Anderson, Kristian.
        Days like these : even in the darkest moments, light can shine through / Kristian
Anderson with Rachel Anderson.
        p. cm.
        ISBN 978-0-310-32583-3 (hardcover)
        1. Anderson, Kristian — Health. 2. Intestines — Cancer — Patients — Australia —
Biography. I. Anderson, Rachel. II. Title.
RC280.I5A53 2013
616.99′4340092 — dc23
        [B]   2012040550

All Scripture quotations, unless otherwise indicated, are taken from The Holy Bible, *New International Version®, NIV®.* Copyright © 1973, 1978, 1984, 2011 by Biblica, Inc.™ Used by permission. All rights reserved worldwide.

Scripture quotations marked MSG are taken from *The Message.* Copyright © 1993, 1994, 1995, 1996, 2000, 2001, 2002. Used by permission of NavPress Publishing Group.

Scripture quotations marked ESV are taken from *The Holy Bible, English Standard Version,* copyright © 2001 by Crossway Bibles, a division of Good News Publishers. Used by permission. All rights reserved.

Scripture quotations marked CEV are taken from the *Contemporary English Version.* Copyright © 1995 by American Bible Society. Used by permission.

Any Internet addresses (websites, blogs, etc.) and telephone numbers in this book are offered as a resource. They are not intended in any way to be or imply an endorsement by Zondervan, nor does Zondervan vouch for the content of these sites and numbers for the life of this book.

First published in Sydney, Australia, by HarperCollins Publishers Australia Pty Limited in 2012. This edition is published by arrangement with HarperCollins Publishers Australia Pty Limited.

Cover design: Matt Stanton, HarperCollins Design Studio
*Cover photography: from the video Kristian made for Rachel's birthday with the help of
    Keith Rodger and the team at South Sydney Media.*
Interior photography: Kristian and Rachel Anderson
Interior design: Matt Stanton, HarperCollins Design Studio; Katherine Lloyd, The DESK

Printed in the United States of America

13 14 15 16 17 18 /DCI/ 23 22 21 20 19 18 17 16 15 14 13 12 11 10 9 8 7 6 5 4 3 2 1

For Cody Israel and Jakob Judah.
It was all for you.

Contents

A Note from Rachel Anderson

Ring the bells that still can ring
Forget your perfect offering
There is a crack in everything
That's how the light gets in

LEONARD COHEN, "ANTHEM"

My name is Rachel Anderson, and I am Kristian Anderson's wife. I will not say "was," even though Kristian left this life on January 2, 2012.

Kristian was my husband; the father of our two boys, Cody and Jakob; a television editor; a musician; and a man of faith. Through the last two years of his life, Kristian battled cancer in his bowel and liver. His way of keeping his friends and family updated with what was happ ening with his cancer battle and in our world was through his blog, "How the Light Gets In" (www.howthelightgetsin.net). In choosing the name, Kristian was inspired by Leonard Cohen's lyrics; he said that the words seemed like a good fit for him at that time in his life.

As it turned out, Kristian's blog was seen by people far beyond the immediate circle of those who loved him. More than a quarter of a million people paid a visit from all around the globe. He had many visitors from Australia, the United States, and New Zealand, as well as more than 150 other countries. In the week he died, there were over 450,000 hits on the blog.

Through his last months here, Kristian worked on writing a book that he could leave behind for Cody, Jakob, and me, drawing on words and photos from his blog. Now that he is gone, it seemed that one way we could honor his memory was to make sure this book came to be.

So here it is. I hope it will be a blessing to the many who loved and supported Kristian through the time he was with us.

Rachel Anderson,
February 2012

Let Me Bring You Up to Speed

ERASE AND REWIND

Let me bring you up to speed.

I have cancer.

In the bowel and liver.

I am thirty-four years old.

I have a beautiful wife and two boys under three years of age.

NO NEWS IS GOOD NEWS?

Friday, October 2

After traveling to the United States for a friend's wedding during the last week of September 2009, I arrived back in Sydney with the usual jetlag associated with a thirteen-hour flight. I didn't think much of it and continued on with my work schedule.

Went in to work to tidy up the editing office. Did a little bit of file archiving. Shut the office down at the mains, as I was about to start an eight-week contract as one of the editors on *Come Dine With Me Australia* at another editing facility at Fox Studios.

Saturday, October 3

Headed out to do some demo recordings with a young Newcastle band at The Grove Studios. Tracking was basic but successful, and we got what we wanted.

"YOU GO SEE THE DOCTOR, DAD"

Those were the words of my three-year-old son, Cody. He had asked me if I was OK, as he often does, and I had replied that I had a sore tummy.

Monday, October 5

Public holiday. Woke up at 12:00 a.m. with what I thought was a nasty stitch in my side. You know, the kind you get when you go out running. Quite a bit of discomfort but just tried to ignore it. No relief by 5:00 p.m., so off to the doctor's surgery I go, with a stern but loving send-off from Rachel and Cody. Went to Warringah Mall Medical Centre and, for the first time in ten years, got a doctor who seemed genuinely interested in treating me. Turns out he is taking an online songwriting course at Berklee College of Music in Boston and is a bit of a music/audio nut. We got along great. Doc says I may have deep vein thrombosis due to recent air travel, but since I mentioned I have also been getting a little blood in my bowel movements, he refers me to emergency and another specialist.

6:00 p.m.: I am admitted to Manly Hospital, scans are ordered, and by 11:00 p.m., it is determined I have a blood clot on my lungs. I am given blood-thinning medication immediately and ordered to stay overnight.

D-DAY (DIAGNOSIS DAY)

From here on out, everything in our lives has been separated by this day—before diagnosis/after diagnosis. This is a marker we can't ignore, much as we would like to.

Tuesday, October 6

After a night of almost no sleep (emergency ward, lights on all night), I chat with the nurses who advise me my treatment will be simple, just a daily injection of Warfarin (blood thinner) and a daily blood sample. Six months' worth should do it. Resign myself to the fact that I will have to do it and decide to discharge myself, against doctor's wishes.

Q: Why would I discharge myself if the doc said not to?

A: I work for myself and was already missing the first day of an eight-week contract. Not a good look for a new client, even though they were aware of the situation and very understanding.

Tried to check out but then nearly passed out so was ordered to stay.

Because I tried to leave, they gave my room to another patient, and now I'm sitting in the corridor. Rachel arrives about an hour later with Jakob in tow; Cody is at kindergarten.

The specialist asks to speak with us. Says there's been a mistake. They use voice recognition software to get the reports done, and the software thought it heard "blood clot present" when in actual fact the doctor said "no blood clot present." Sorry about that, but while you're here, we noticed something unusual at the bottom of the lung scan, on your liver. There are lesions there that concern us, and we'd like to do another scan. We're pretty sure that with the symptoms you're presenting, you have cancer. But we need to check it to be sure.

You know that feeling you got in your stomach when you were young and you got caught doing something naughty, that feeling of impending doom? Yeah, that one. I got it right about here. Rach and I just sit there while Jakob gets into all the things a one-year-old kid loves to get into. So glad he's oblivious.

If you've spent time in a hospital, you know it involves a lot of waiting around. By the time we get all this info, it's time to get Cody from kindy, so Rach heads out to pick him up. As it turns out, today is the day Rachel's parents arrive from Auckland. They're here to compete in the cycling in the Masters Games (which aren't for a few days yet), so Rach drops Cody off with Nanna and Poppa, and Cody thinks he's in heaven.

Sitting by yourself in a little hospital waiting room is not fun when there are less-serious items on the table, let alone the possibility of cancer. It's not a good place for me to be by myself and in the eerie soundscape of the ER, I begin to pray. I have no eloquent words to use. No lofty prayers to the Almighty. Just two words:

God, help.

They're ready for me to go in for the next scan, so I drink a liter of oral contrast and lie down while they prep the scanner. The phone rings; it's Rachel's ringtone ("Take on Me" by A-ha; I wanted to use "I Touch Myself" by the Divinyls, but she said she would never call me again if I did), and I lose it. I can't help but be frightened, and on the other end of that phone call is my wife. The thought of leaving her and the boys is too much. Trying to keep still for the scan, but my body is heaving from the sobs. Finally get it together long enough for the scanner to do its thing and then get wheeled back to my room.

Rachel arrives. More sobbing. Both of us. The sound echoing off the tiny room with high ceilings. Jude, the Scottish doctor, comes in to take my cannula out so I can go home. She knows what's going on; I can tell by the look in her eyes and by the way she gently touches my arm. Specialists in another room down the hall are gathered around my scans. Various noddings and so on. Doc comes in and says it's cancer. No primary in the liver, so they're guessing that one is in the bowel. Go home; rest up; see the surgeon in a few days.

Rachel drives her car home, and I get into mine. Halfway home I lose it again, and the road becomes blurry. No subtle prayers, no dignified utterances, no sacred recitals—just weeping ... shouting.

God, help.

IN SICKNESS AND IN HEALTH

Rachel and I can't look at each other without bursting into tears. Trying to keep it together in front of the boys is difficult. We don't want them to detect any upset, because there's no way we can make them understand the gravity of what's happening. We went to sleep crying and woke up the same way. I felt Rachel put her arms around me during the night, and then I felt her body shaking from the tears.

It's just not real. This is not our life.

JUST RELAX

I can't remember the date, but we ended up back at the surgeon's office. He was very matter-of-fact, which I prefer, and told us what we were dealing with: cancer. He orders a colonoscopy and gives me some PicoPrep, which is basically a really fast way to empty the bowels before he jams a camera up my bum and takes a look around.

Any male who is happily heterosexual will understand the cringe factor attached to this procedure. Needless to say, I am not looking forward to it.

OH, DIGNITY, WHERE ART THOU?

Friday, October 9

Back at Manly Hospital for the dignity-destroying colonoscopy.

9:00 a.m.: All ready to go, something injected into my arm, oxygen mask on ... feeling sleepy.

Close eyes.

Open eyes.

Ask when they're going to get it over with. Nurse says it's now 10:30 a.m., and the procedure has been completed successfully.

For all I know, I was kidnapped by aliens and probed for an hour and a half before being delivered back to the very same position I was in before the kidnapping. I'm not sore at all, so I guess they must have been gentle. Anyway, better to not dwell on that one. Anesthetic wears off, and Rach drives me home. Grateful the hospital is only ten minutes' drive, via Manly beach. At least I have nice scenery while I contemplate my "probing."

EVEN THOUGH I WALK THROUGH THE VALLEY OF THE SHADOW OF DEATH

We're back in the surgeon's office.

Yep, it's bowel cancer. It's about forty-five centimeters up my bowel and is about two centimeters in size, wrapped around 75 percent of the colon. Judging by the size and usual growth times of these sorts of things, it's been there for about eighteen months. This explains why it has been hard to get bowel movements happening of late. It has also spread to the liver, but we knew that.

Wonderful.

I am referred to an oncologist and we go home. Strangely enough, feeling all right.

Even though I walk through the valley of the shadow
of death,
I will fear no evil,
for you are with me.

PSALM 23:4 CEV

I now know what it means to walk through the valley of the shadow of death. But the thing about a shadow is that it is vaporized by light.

First John 1:5 reads:

This is the message we have heard from him and declare to you: God is light; in him there is no darkness at all.

As I emailed a friend:

For some reason my faith is surging when I am normally quite melancholy. I sense a battle ahead, but I also sense a victory. I'm frightened of the medical processes ahead. My body is going to go through hell, not to mention my mind – but I have hope. Real hope. I'm going to make it out the other side of this, and there will be tales of miracles. It's time for me to stand up and be counted.

What poor research my enemy has undertaken! His recon team should be hung, drawn, and quartered! What terrible destruction I will bring to his doorstep. What violence I will unleash against him.

Don't you know who I am? Don't you know what you've just awoken? Don't you know who fights for me?

You will regret the day you picked a fight with me. You can count on it.

> "Because he loves me," says the LORD, "I will rescue him; I will protect him, for he acknowledges my name. He will call upon me, and I will answer him; I will be with him in trouble, I will deliver him and honor him. With long life I will satisfy him and show him my salvation." (Psalm 91:14 – 16)

ONCOLOGY

That's a word I never thought would pass my lips.

Oncologist.

Arrive at Manly Hospital again, head up to the oncology ward. Very quiet here. Just a few people sitting around receiving their chemotherapy. This will be me in a few weeks' time.

We go in and start getting some explanations. One of the

hardest things through all of this is the waiting for confirmations and/or information. I feel as though I have been hung over a cliff with nothing but a thread to hold me up, swinging in the breeze.

Waiting.

More waiting.

Yes, no, maybe.

Bloody hell.

The surgeon won't comment on the oncology side, and the oncologist won't comment on the surgery side. OK, fair enough. But tell me something.

So we're getting down to the nuts and bolts now. Chemotherapy. Three months' worth. Once every two weeks.

A TRIP TO "THE BANK"

With chemotherapy confirmed, Rachel and I have to make a decision on some "family planning" issues.

Meaning, Rachel wants more kids, and there's a fifty-fifty chance the chemo will knock my little swimmers out of action. It's too great a risk to take for us, so we're referred to IVF Australia and organize a "deposit."

Now, I have seen this sort of thing in movies and heard stories about it, but nothing prepared me for what I was about to experience. We rock up to this unassuming little building on the Pacific Highway in Greenwich on a Saturday morning, en route to my nan's ninetieth birthday party no less, and I head inside. Rach and the boys wait in the car. Up to the first floor, and there's only women at reception.

Great. As if this wasn't already awkward enough for me.

Fill in all the forms, permissions, power of attorney, etc., in case something happens to me, and then I am introduced to the scientist. Who happens to be a not unattractive Asian woman about my age. It just gets better.

So we fill in some more forms, and the terminology on these forms is making me blush a bit—but, hey, it's for a scientist, right? It's all for science. The camera up the behind and now this—all for science. Can someone nominate me for a Nobel Prize in physiology or medicine? Geez, if Barack Obama can get the Peace Prize, then surely I can get some kind of concession here?

Anyway, the lovely scientist leads me to my cubicle, and in I go. Based on what I have been told, I am expecting a pile of porno mags, but no. The digital age has come to sperm banking, and there's not a magazine in sight. Instead there stands a pearly white Samsung LCD monitor, all neatly cabled and connected to an AV socket in the wall. Quality installation. Out of curiosity, I press the power button. Maybe the Weather Channel or MTV?

No.

Just what you'd expect. Off with the TV.

Anyway, you know the rest. I did what I had to do and got out of there quick smart. I was a little anxious about returning. The doc said I'd need to go three times to get enough stems to be viable. The thought of doing it twice more was a little unsettling. But not to worry, the scientist called me back a few hours later and said that she normally likes to receive twenty stems for a viable freeze and I gave her nineteen. So I don't need to go back. Woohoo!

I've told Rachel she better not even look at my groin or she could get pregnant. Maybe those Superman undies weren't so ostentatious after all?

Anyway, as you were.

FALSE START

I was supposed to start chemotherapy today. It was to be a long day of education, inserting the PICC line (like a permanent drip line for the drugs) in my arm, and then the first round of drugs. It turns out the PICC line would be a real hassle. Constantly needing to change the dressing, can't go swimming at all (it's warm here now and the beach is so beautiful in the mornings), but the biggest issue for me was that there was so much external guff that it would be quite difficult to be around the boys and not have an accident. All these bits and pieces hanging off my arm would have been a huge dangling carrot for Jakob, who loves to play with anything and everything. He doesn't understand *no* yet so the only way to keep the PICC line safe would be by seriously limiting my contact with him. And that's not gonna happen.

So we opted for the port catheter (or portacath) instead, which is basically a silicon injection pad inserted under my skin and a catheter that goes directly to the vein required for the chemotherapy. It requires a brief surgery to have it installed, but after that it can stay there for years. I can function totally as per normal (if indeed I ever was normal), and the port is really low maintenance in comparison to the PICC. It's also totally invisible to the untrained eye, which will mean Cody won't notice any weird cables coming out of Daddy's arm. Another plus.

I'm a little bummed as I really wanted to get this thing underway, but ultimately this will make the chemo easier to deal with, so I will wait. The other bummer is that it will change my on/off cycle by a week. My sister-in-law is coming over for a week in November on what would have been my "on" week. She's a doctor, and I was kinda looking forward to her coming to the oncology ward with me to check it all out. Anyway … it's OK, I guess. Met another doctor today too—the vascular surgeon who will implant the port. He makes about the seventh doctor in two weeks.

My mother is here for a week, so we have someone to look after the kids tonight. It's pretty rare that we get to go out at night these days without the kids, so we're going to see a movie. I know it's not the most romantic of evenings, and it's cheap-date Tuesday, so it will likely be packed. But, for me, anywhere alone with Rach is pretty special. It will also be nice to go out and forget about things for a couple hours.

NOT JUST ANY PORT IN A STORM

I spent yesterday back in the company of the wonderful staff at Manly Hospital. I'm not being sarcastic either. They're truly amazing people. From the admissions staff to the nurses to the surgeons, everyone cares. The Australian media has really got it wrong with all their hospital bashing. And the best part? It's all free. Medicare is taking care of everything. What kind of incredible country do I live in where all my medical costs are covered by the government? One of the drugs required for chemotherapy is $5,000 a month by itself! So if you have an inkling that Australia is not the lucky country anymore, let me tell you now, you couldn't be more off the mark. Anyone who lives here is truly blessed.

It was a good day to be inside, as it was gray and overcast outside, so off we went to get the portacath installed. I headed up with Rach at 11:00 a.m., got prepped, and then just waited. Rach headed off to do some stuff, and the nurses told her they would call when I was ready for pickup. Again, in with the cannula, on with the oxygen mask, and a guy came and drew an arrow on my chest. Kind of like a "this is where you cut him open" marker. No kidding. Thankfully everyone in the operating room can read map directions. When I woke up, I was sore in the right place.

They really hammered me with the anesthetic. I've never been so groggy coming out of an operation before. I was aware that my speech was quite impaired, less than half the speed I usually talk, and my mouth was very dry. It's quite a trip when you're trying your hardest to open your eyes and they just won't respond. By the time I finally opened up, it was close to 7:00 p.m. My mum was home watching the boys, so Rachel arrived not long after and I was discharged.

When we got home, Cody was very happy to see me, but he had been told Daddy was very sore on his shoulder and to be gentle with him, not to hurt him. Bless his little heart, when I asked him for a cuddle he started forward but then obviously remembered what he'd been told and pulled back. "Nooooo," he said. "I don't hurt me on my shoulder. You got sore shoulder, Dad." Cody gets his you/me muddled up sometimes, but I knew what he meant. I showed him the "hospital stickers," which is what he calls the bandages. He looked at them and said, "I like your cool stickers, Dad!"

Kristian holds Jakob
during a chemo trip.

It's nice to know that in the middle of all of this, there are people who love me just because. I can't imagine what it must be like to get this kind of news and have no one to lean on.

I walk around my house and see all of the boys' toys scattered all over the floor, and I think to myself, *How beautiful!*

I see one of Rachel's *Understanding Chemotherapy* books left on the bed and know the woman I married is educating herself so she can fight beside me.

When Rachel and I were married, I promised her in my vows that I would fight for her. I never imagined it would be this kind of fight, but I will not let her down. I will fight this cancer with every ounce of strength I have, and when I have none left and can walk no farther, I will rest and let my God carry me.

> ... *those who hope in the LORD*
>   *will renew their strength.*
> *They will soar on wings like eagles;*

they will run and not grow weary,
they will walk and not be faint.

Isaiah 40:31

THIS ISN'T KANSAS ANYMORE, TOTO

The past week has been ... intense.

It started last Monday with a five-hour infusion at the hospital.

To give you an idea of the toxicity of the drugs I am receiving, the nurses wear elbow-length rubber gloves, face masks, and full-body gowns just to handle the drugs in their bags. The drugs don't at any time leave their bags except to enter my body through a tube. So while the nurses go to great care to protect themselves from any kind of exposure to the drugs, they freely pump me full of them. If that wasn't enough to add a few more gray hairs to the scalp, further research revealed that chemotherapy has its origins in chemical warfare. It was discovered by accident during World War II, when doctors were performing autopsies on soldiers killed with mustard gas. Over the years, it has been developed and refined into the treatment I am receiving now.

This is serious business. They're actually killing parts of my body to get to the tumors.

There is one word that I think describes chemotherapy: *Violent.*

I actually felt OK the day of my initial infusion and the day after, though a little queasy. I even did a full day's work the day after.

But the next day, that's when I got hit. Nausea, vomiting,

fever, sweating, dehydration, and—your friend and mine—diarrhea. I also had the hiccups for fifteen hours straight.

So I drive myself from the edit suite to the hospital to see the oncology nurse.

(Mental note: Don't drive when about to pass out. I'm sure it voids something in the fine print on my insurance policy.)

Arrive at the hospital, nurses look horrified, and I'm immediately admitted to the ER. Then, following a variety of tests, I am told I'm not going home and am moved to my own room for the night. Small mercies: my own room with a sunset view out over Sydney Harbour. But I still want to go home.

No, you're staying put.

Hospital is all about waiting, and it's hard to stay positive when your mind has such a dull environment to go wild in. Suffice to say, it was not a pleasant night for me, despite the stunning view out my window. My mind continually wandered to Rachel, Cody, and Jakob. In the loneliness and darkness, the fear begins to talk to me, mocking me. My mind is besieged by all sorts of fatalistic imagery, and the tears come like a flood.

Then something clicks inside me.

No.

It is written:

He was looked down on and passed over,
a man who suffered, who knew pain firsthand.
One look at him and people turned away.
We looked down on him, thought he was scum.
But the fact is, it was our pains he carried—
our disfigurements, all the things wrong with us.
We thought he brought it on himself,
that God was punishing him for his own failures.

But it was our sins that did that to him,
   that ripped and tore and crushed him—our sins!
He took the punishment, and that made us whole.
   Through his bruises we get healed.

ISAIAH 53:3 MSG

Through His bruises I get healed.

Through His bruises I get healed.

Through His bruises I get healed.

And then the room is flooded with peace and I sleep.

The next day I'm told that the doctors believe I have picked up a bug or infection of some kind. Chemotherapy messes up the immune system, and while I am receiving infusions I will be vulnerable. This just happened to be "really bad luck," according to my oncologist. Future infusions should not affect me so badly. I'm kept another day to be safe and then sent home on Friday afternoon.

Kristian got an infection after his first chemo treatment and had to spend a few days in the hospital. Cody and Jakob came to visit.

When I get home, Cody is at kindergarten, and Jakob is super happy to see me, and we have the most awesome cuddles on the couch. Every second is treasure beyond words.

I can now feel a seismic shift going on inside me. It's one thing to say "I will fight this" when it's just a diagnosis on paper. It's another thing entirely to sustain that focus while you're in the thick of the battle, bleeding from the fury of the fight. This fight is as much physical as it is emotional and spiritual. You can't stare into the face of your own mortality and walk away without being profoundly and irreversibly changed.

This is as real as it gets.

My body will survive this assassination attempt, of that I am sure, but the old Kristian, the precancer me, is dead.

HOLDING PATTERN

I'm agitated and cranky, and I don't know why.

I hate it. I mean, I *really* hate it.

I'm so tired most of the time that I can only do things in short bursts. Any sudden loud noises echo through my brain like a firecracker in a bathroom. I'm finding it very difficult to order my thoughts at all; it's like trying to catch a fly buzzing around the room. I'm short-tempered with the boys, which is killing me, because I love them so much; and on top of that, I feel as though Rachel has to do everything, and it's not fair to her. Our household only works because of her, but now she has to deal with my mood swings as well, on top of everything else.

Does she complain? Of course not. She is not your average, run-of-the-mill woman.

She's the best one of the best ones.

I can't work anywhere near the level I could before, so my earning capacity is way down. I'm being up-front with people who call me for work and telling them that I am in the middle of chemotherapy for cancer. On my "off" week, I'm fine and can work no problem, but my "on" week is a complete write-off. If they'd like to book me for my off week, I promise I won't drop dead on them.

They don't call back.

It's my job to provide for my family, and I feel like I'm not pulling my weight. I feel like a big, fat lump of lard sitting lazily on the couch or flat on my back in bed, too tired to do anything.

My oncology nurse keeps telling me to listen to my body. If you feel tired, then sleep. It's the body's way of telling you it needs to rest, to regenerate. You're being pumped full of toxic drugs. It's OK to rest. And I know she's right, but in the seventeen years since I graduated high school and started working, this is the longest break from work I have ever had. It's going on six weeks now, and I'm really struggling with the need to contribute and the need to get better. I loathe waste. Wasted time, wasted energy, wasted resources. I know that my getting better is not a waste. Far from it. But I've got plans, things I want to do. Things I need to do, and sitting around on my arse all day just really rubs me the wrong way.

BLOOD BROTHERS

More and more I am learning that this life is not about the things you have or even the things you do.

Precancer I felt I was defined by my job, my skills, and the outcomes they produced for myself, my family, or my clients. I prided myself on being able to deliver, no matter what. I was good at my job. Very good. I surrounded myself with coworkers who were just as good, or better, in their area of expertise and, by doing so, made impossible deadlines without sacrificing quality.

If it's true that a smart guy knows what he's dumb at, then I was Einstein. I knew my weaknesses and surrounded myself with people who were strong in those areas.

I still believe in excellence and a good work ethic, but I have realized that life is not what you have or what you do. That kind of thinking is nothing but a fleeting vanity.

It's about who walks beside you on your way.

You can surround yourself with all different kinds of people, but it's only when you're being hammered by the storm that you learn not only what's inside yourself but what's inside those surrounding you.

Like my friend who fasted and prayed for three days immediately after I called him with the news. Or my other friend who said he would fly to Sydney from the other side of the country if I needed any help at all. Or my other friend who stays up at night praying for me and my family, asking God how he can help. Or my other friend who came around to our house late at night to pray with us once we got the news, even after he'd had a long day at work. Or my other friend who last night sent me a photo from his studio. He's working away in the wee hours of the night, but right in front of him as he works is a list of things he is asking God for on my behalf.

My family means everything to me. Rachel, Cody, and Jakob are my heart and soul. Nothing can ever take their place.

But next to them are my blood brothers from around the country and around the world.

My generals.

They stand with me and are not afraid to fight in my place.

I am deeply, deeply honored to have such people in my life. I cannot even begin to describe the intensity of my gratitude.

But the stars are burnin' bright like some
mystery uncovered.
I'll keep movin' through the dark with you
in my heart,
my blood brother.

BRUCE SPRINGSTEEN, "BLOOD BROTHERS"

THE NUMBERS

I had my regular meeting with my oncologist yesterday. I quite enjoy visiting him. He's a nice guy.

We sit down in his office, and he asks me how I'm feeling. I tell him I'm feeling good. He asks about the side effects of the treatment and if I'm having trouble with them. I tell him that except for some hiccups, some reflux on the days I'm still hooked up to the 5-FU (my take-home drug), and general (heavy) tiredness, I'm not experiencing any noticeable side effects. No vomiting, no nausea, no secondary illnesses.

He smiles. Good.

He then tells me it's quite remarkable that my body is doing this well. These drugs are potent, and I am getting a heavy dose. He tells me the treatment is an important part of what we're doing here, but equally as important is my mental state, how I view the cancer, and "what you have on the inside of you—what you're made of."

I then ask him how my blood work is. I want to know.

As I understand it, the tumors expel proteins (carcino-embryonic antigens, or CEA) into the bloodstream that are different to any others. These are my cancer markers. These numbers let us know how things are progressing and whether or not my body is responding to the treatment.

Before I began chemotherapy, my CEA readings (bloodstream) were 4,058 ug/L (that's micrograms per liter). A normal, cancer-free person has less than three.

After my first infusion, they rose to 4,323. This sounds bad, but it is not uncommon as the tumors often surge after first being hit. They're kinda pissed off, so they react by swelling. It's very likely that they surged upwards of 5,000 before coming back down by the time of the second blood test.

As of today, my CEA markers are 3,470—a 20 percent decline.

My bowels also have their own markers—CA 19-9. Pre-chemo they were 88.4 U/mL (units per milliliter). A normal, cancer-free person has less than thirty-seven.

After my first infusion, they dropped to 79, and as of today, they are 68.9, a 22 percent drop.

In short, I'm a responder.

This is good news. The tumors are taking a hit after only two infusions. The blood results also show that my liver is functioning 100 percent—perfectly. More good news, considering it was covered in tumors last time we looked.

After we're done chatting, I get up to leave, shake the doc's hand, and go home.

It takes three hours to wipe the smile off my face.

For those of you who have taken up the call to pray for me, this is for you. You are making a difference. Your prayers are powerful and effective.

Please don't stop. My life depends on it.

After his first chemo treatment, Kristian had to be set up for a bolus infusion for forty-eight hours, which slowly infused one of the chemo drugs into his system. Judging by his expression, he is unimpressed.

WAR CRY

I'm writing this to honor my wife, Rachel. I've just had round three of my chemo and thought it best to get this down "on paper," as it were, before I head into the next few days of dream-like existence as the drugs work their way through my system.

When I was single and stupid, I asked God to make sure I never married a New Zealander or a singer. I have no idea why I said that, but it's true, I did. I'm so glad He saw through the stupidity of my request and decided to ignore it. Instead,

At Dee Why beach, not long after we started dating; Kristian met
my family when they came over from New Zealand.

He brought me an incredible woman who was, in fact, both of the things I thought I wanted to avoid. How right He was, and how grateful I am.

Rach loves her homeland, Aotearoa—land of the long, white cloud—and over the years I, too, have grown to love it. In particular, the Maori culture—it is all at once beautiful and ferocious, passionate and noble, creative and soulful.

So, as a skinny white guy from Australia, I'll put my best *haka* face on and stand up in defense of my *whanau*, my family, and say this:

Ka mate, ka mate—I die, I die
Ka ora' ka ora'—I live, I live!
Ka mate, ka mate—I die, I die!
Ka ora' ka ora'—I live, I live!
Tenei te tangata puhuruhuru—
  This is the man
Nana i tiki mai whakawhiti te ra—
  Who caused the sun to shine again for me
Upane, upane—Up the ladder, up the ladder
Upane kaupane—Up to the top
Whiti te ra!—The sun shines!
Hi!—Rise!

"KA MATE" HAKA

If I could literally stand in front of my cancer, this is what I would do; this is what it would see. I think the All Blacks' rugby legend Tana Umaga does it best—and I like to think the angels going into battle for me look a little like him before they bring some pain to my enemy's doorstep.

Game on.

THANKSGIVING

Back in January this year, the house next door to us was sold, and the family that lived there moved out. The new owner was keen to meet his new neighbors, so on Australia Day, he threw a street party. Free beer, free barbecue, and a jumping castle for the kids. The whole street rocked up, and for a lot of us it was our first introduction to each other. On that day, we met Tony and Brenda and their family from Minnesota. They were not only new to our street but also to the country. We got talking, and it turns out they recently started attending our church too. (That's what happens in a big church; you often don't notice new people.) Since that day, we have become great friends. Their generosity and hospitality are humbling, and we're truly honored to call them our friends.

On Friday night, we were invited over for Thanksgiving dinner. I wasn't feeling so hot, so Rach went over with the

Early in Kristian's cancer journey, Tony and Brenda gave us a weekend away in the Blue Mountains.

boys. This current round of chemotherapy has been a little more taxing than the last one. More nausea and a lot more tiredness, plus it's been quite hot, so I ended up making an appearance an hour or so later, after I'd woken up from a nap. We had a great time, and there was some amazing food, including a pumpkin pie that was something else—all home cooked.

Tony and Brenda's family have a tradition of writing—in permanent marker on a big white cloth—all the things they are thankful for that year, and they invited Rachel and me to write on it too.

It got me thinking. What am I thankful for?

I came up with a list a mile long. Rachel, Cody, and Jakob were obviously up there on top, as well as all of our friends and family, who are upholding us in prayer and supporting us with meals and finances.

But ultimately, I came to the conclusion that I had so much to be thankful for I just couldn't write it all down.

Inside my body is something that has no other purpose but to kill me. It's called cancer, and it's a really nasty piece of work. But instead of bitching and moaning, I find myself waking up every day thankful for one simple fact:

I'm alive.

WHEN THE WAR IS OVER

There are some things in this life that I will never understand. As long I wear this frail coating of flesh and blood, as long as the fragility of my own humanity covers me, I will never understand.

This morning I got news that some good friends of ours lost their little girl. There had been complications while she was still in the womb, and surgery was scheduled for this morning. But it wasn't to be. She came in the night, far too early, and only graced us with her presence for an hour before being gently carried to the Father's side in the arms of an angel.

To me, this is the definition of unfair.

Is it fair for me to have cancer?

Maybe.

Depends on who you speak to.

I'm thirty-four, an adult, and my hands are dirty.

But not this little one. She was innocent. As innocent as it gets.

I can't even begin to imagine the pain that is enveloping our friends right now. And try as I might, there's nothing I can do to ease it for them. One day I'm sure I will be able to comprehend all of this, but that day is not today.

How long, O Lord, how long?

Son of David ... have mercy.

FROM RACHEL

When Kristian first went to the hospital and we still thought he had a pulmonary embolism, I was annoyed at having to pick him up. I had plans for that day: it was a kindy day for Cody, and I wanted to tidy the house, because Mum and Dad were arriving from New Zealand. Kristian just said when he called from the hospital, "Can you come up and bring Jake with you? It's a bit lonely here." So I rearranged my plans. When I dropped Cody at kindy, I told the boys that Daddy was in the hospital with a blood clot in his lungs but he should be fine.

Jakey was crawling on the floor in emergency while I was sitting with Kristian. Then a lovely lady came and sat chatting with us; I didn't realize at the time that she was a doctor. She explained that there had been a mistake and Kristian didn't have a blood clot. Then she said to him, "But we're seeing some funny things on your liver, so I need to ask you a few questions." I immediately got that feeling in my stomach that something wasn't right.

Kristian freaked out a little bit then, but at that point I had to go because Jake was due to take a nap, and my parents were arriving. As soon as Mum and Dad had got in, I went straight back up to the hospital. Kristian had just had his second scan, and we were sitting in this little waiting room, and then the doctor came in. As soon as I saw his face, I stood and said, "Do you want to sit down?" and he replied, "No, no, you sit down."

He told us, "We've done the scan; we've seen some thickening in the bowel, and there are some fairly ominous-looking shadows on the liver, and we think it might be cancer."

We were both just devastated. Then Kristian got a phone call from the people he was supposed to start editing with on *Come Dine With Me Australia*. This woman rang, and he had to say to her, "I'm sorry, I can't work; I've got cancer." Hearing the words out loud was so awful.

Those first few days were hideous. It was like your worst nightmare. Even so, after Kristian had had the colonoscopy, I looked at him and said, "I feel OK. I feel like now we know what it is, and we can deal with it." And he was the same, saying, "We can do this; we can fight it." We knew it was serious — cancer on its own is serious enough — but we didn't realize how critical it was.

We thought because it had only spread to his liver that he was just stage 2, when actually, at diagnosis, he was stage 4, which is as bad as it gets. And I think it was probably a good thing that we were blissfully unaware of the reality. Kristian was told he'd have three months of chemo, and we thought that would be it. We would get through a few months of chemo every two weeks and have another scan, and then if the cancer was still there, we would have options. He could have a liver resection, which would cut out the chunks of cancer, and it would grow back cancer free. Then if there was more cancer, they could cut out some more. It was going to be tough, but we'd be all right. That's what we thought. And I'm glad: if we had known how serious it was right from the start, we would have lived quite differently and not as well.

We hadn't had our hopes dashed yet, and that's why I wanted to save some sperm. I was desperate for more children. I'd always wanted four. We had one window of opportunity before Kristian started chemo and when I was ovulating, and I begged him to just try. I said that if it's meant to be, we'll have a baby, and if not, we'll bank some sperm and worry about it later. But Kristian didn't want to try. If he died, he said, he didn't want to leave me alone with three children; it would be too much.

In hindsight he made the right decision. If we had gone ahead, I wouldn't have been able to get back to work as I did. I don't know how we would have survived financially, but as it was, I worked for a year and a half while Kristian was ill. The school where I had been working called me because they urgently needed a science teacher. I kept saying no and they kept calling, and eventually I said, "If I can get child care lined up, then I'll do it." And child care fell into place. Work proved to be exactly what I needed for my sanity. The boys were happy at day care, and I was able to go to this completely different place where I wasn't in cancer land.

I was essentially solo parenting for the greater part of that journey. It was lonely and it was horrible, but it meant that I knew I could do the day-to-day stuff on my own. I'm very grateful that God allowed things to happen the way they did. Especially toward the end, when it was very serious, I knew I would be all right; I'd miss Kristian, but I'd cope. And it was important for Kristian to know that I would be all right as well.

2
Going the Distance

DRESS CODE

December 7, 2009

I go in for round four of my chemotherapy tomorrow. To be honest, I don't want to go. Not because I don't want to get better but because the path to getting better makes me feel pretty crappy for about a week. It's a small price to pay, but it's still a high cost in comparison to, say, the flu or a cold. Either of those is treated by some brightly colored and easily ingested tablets. Not so for my disease.

I'm not getting any of the side effects the doctors warned me about, which is amazing in and of itself. But it messes with my mind a lot. And I can smell the drugs seeping from my pores the entire week, and that smell makes me feel physically ill.

I am anxious, however, to see the results from my last set of blood work. It's been two weeks, and I'm more than curious.

I've had a good week this week. I've worked four days out of seven and even established a new client in the process, who was very understanding and unbelievably flexible with regard to what weeks I could and could not work. The entire company

43

was so nice to me and so accommodating. I was quite surprised, but not as surprised as when one of the designers came into my suite and introduced himself.

We got talking, and he asked politely if I could give him some more detail about what I was dealing with when it came to the cancer. Some people feel awkward asking me about it, but truth be told, I have no problem discussing it. It's not something to be ashamed of. This fight was not of my choosing, but as long as it's here, I am most certainly up for it.

Our conversation continued until he asked me if I had "a faith." To which I replied, "Yes, I do. I follow Christ." He immediately smiled and said he knew it, just by the way I was talking about my future in the face of a potentially terminal disease. He then asked if he could pray for me, which I thought was just awesome. So in the quiet of the color-grading suite, with nothing but the sound of fans from various pieces of high-tech gadgetry whirring away in the background, he put his hand on my stomach and began to pray. Not a big, loud prayer. He wasn't trying to conjure anything up. He just quietly asked God to remove the cancer from my body, like he does it every day.

Immediately the room was filled with peace.

I know this peace. I have felt it many times before. It rests on my body like a warm blanket and surrounds me like a soft duvet.

Rest. Comfort. Ease.

It brings all of these and more.

And it got me thinking.

Since being diagnosed with this stupid disease, the support and help that have come our way have been nothing short of amazing. For someone like me, who often spends a lot of time (happily) on my own, mostly oblivious to the things going on around me, it has impacted me deeply to know that so many people care about what happens to me. Unfortunately though, there have been a handful of comments sent my way that just do not sit well with me.

I know their intentions are good and that they genuinely care about my well-being, but when someone says that maybe I should "check my heart" for things like unforgiveness, bitterness, or pride, or perhaps investigate my family line to see if those things (or worse indiscretions) are buried in my family history, as that may be the cause of my cancer—well, I'm sorry, but I just want to flip you the bird.

I am not being punished here. This cancer has not been placed on me as a consequence of something I may or may not have done in the past.

My God does not delight in spiteful retribution. If you think He does, then maybe we're not talking about the same God.

I serve a God who has promised me He will never leave me or forsake me. A God from whom I cannot escape, no matter how hard I run the other way at times. A God whose love for me sent Him willingly to the most barbaric and painful of deaths, crucified on a cross, in my place.

In my place.

John 15:13 states this:

Greater love has no one than this: to lay down one's life for one's friends.

Somehow the concept of someone who willingly died in my place and the idea of that same someone sitting high up in the sky zapping naughty people with terminal diseases just do not gel. Not now, not ever.

When I was first diagnosed, I called up one of my best friends and we went out for coffee. He told me he had been praying about the situation the night before and had asked God why this was happening. He felt the answer was this:

> *Walking down the street, Jesus saw a man blind from birth. His disciples asked, "Rabbi, who sinned: this man or his parents, causing him to be born blind?" Jesus said, "You're asking the wrong question. You're looking for someone to blame. There is no such cause–effect here. Look instead for what God can do."*
>
> JOHN 9:1–3 MSG

So while I understand that these people are on my side, the way they've gone about expressing it makes me recoil violently.

This idea has been floating around in my head since day one, so here it is—my line in the sand:

When you come to me or my family, there is now a dress code in effect. Come to us wearing Faith and Hope, and you will be warmly welcomed. Come to us wearing Fear and Doubt, and you will be politely asked to leave. This dress code will be strictly enforced.

No exceptions.

This is quite literally life or death for me.

This is not some Saturday afternoon paintball fun. This is akin to landing on the beaches of Normandy. My enemy has established a strong hold on my body. Not happy to just mess up my bowel, it marched on my liver. Statistically speaking, my condition is not a good place to be. For me to entertain the thought of anything other than a victory here is to concede defeat, and I may as well go and lie down in a corner somewhere and wait to die.

Let me tell you this now: *I will not lie down.*

I will fight this thing until it is dead. The only one dying around here is cancer. Kristian Anderson will die an old man, peacefully, in his sleep.

How do I know this? Because I know who my God is and what I mean to Him.

For anyone who believes that God is a cranky old man, looking to dish out punishment on us poor, unsuspecting mortals, let me tell you now — He is not like that.

Love is not like that.

LIGHT UP THE NIGHT

I'm struggling tonight.

The nausea is hanging around longer than usual.

Longer than usual.

Like any of this is "usual."

The smell of the drugs is seeping out of my pores, making me want to puke, and — to be really honest — I'm feeling quite emotional.

Part of my way of dealing with this disease is to not give it any more credit than it deserves. I don't dwell on it any more than I need to. I treat this cancer as an adversary. There is not a shred of diplomacy here: it's all-out war, and any weapon is acceptable.

If you have an eye for detail and grammar, you may or may not have noticed that when I use the word *cancer* I don't capitalize it. Some may give it that honor, but I don't give it any respect. It deserves none.

A small thing, I know, but small things make my life beautiful these days.

Maybe I'm emotional because I'm tired. The kind of tired I only discovered existed after I started receiving my infusions. The kind of tired that is not satiated by sleep or rest. The kind of tired that just knocks you on your back and pins you down until it is good and ready to go home.

Maybe.

Maybe I'm emotional because I got some more blood results back on Thursday. They showed my bloodstream markers had dropped another 1,100 points, from 2,777 to 1,666, and that my bowel markers had dropped another 10 points to 52.5—just 15 points off "normal." It's certainly a good reason to get emotional. I cried when the nurse brought them to me. I was amazed and so, so thankful. Maybe that's the reason?

Maybe.

Tonight, in New Zealand, my brother-in-law's band, Mumsdollar, is playing their last ever show after ten years together. Right about now they will be walking onto an Auckland stage to play in front of a sell-out crowd. I was really hoping to get there, and had it been possible to schedule it for my off week, I would have been there for sure. But he and his wife are leaving for the UK in two more days, and they'll be gone for about a year. So it wasn't possible.

I'm listening to their music anyway, as I do, and one of the songs is really getting to me. It's like it was written for me. Like they looked forward in time and saw my illness and then wrote down all the things that would go through my mind once I found I could not continue to live the life I had been living. The life I had before cancer showed up.

This life of mine was once defined
By the kind of things I'd leave behind.
I once was lost, now I'm found.
My rescue came and brought me safe and sound.
Oh, eastern sun you come undone
Over western skies right before my eyes.
All my days I've been finding ways
Of searching for a better way.
Come what may, all my days
I'm searching for a better way back home.
Please slow this ride, it moves too fast.
I've lost control in the past.
These days slip away as evening falls.
And if I hold on too tight, I'll lose it all.
Oh eastern sun you come undone
Over western skies right before my eyes.
All my days I've been finding ways
Of searching for a better way.
Come what may, all my days
Now I'm searching for a better way back home.
Let the past decay, watch it fall away
Far away, there to stay.
No more half black, half white.
No more half wrong, half right.
Now I'm searching for a better way.

MUMSDOLLAR, "BETTER WAY"

Maybe I'm emotional because I finally, truly understand the incredible price that was paid for my life.

Maybe I'm emotional because I realize that — up until this sickness arrived — I had been living a very inward-looking life.

Maybe I'm emotional because I am being given a chance to do better, to find a better way.

"No more half black, half white. No more half wrong, half right."

Heaven is watching. Make it count.

"Better Way" by Mumsdollar

zph.com/dlt/qr1

EVEN CANCER GETS A CHRISTMAS CARD

Tomorrow I go in for round five of my chemotherapy treatment, more blood tests, and hopefully, come Thursday — Christmas Eve — more good news.

I'm happy I'm nearing the end of my treatment, for now at least. So far I've gone through two hundred hours of chemo infusions, and I have another hundred to go. Knowing what lies ahead in the immediate seventy-two hours after the infusion doesn't fill me with a lot of Christmas cheer, but knowing that the cancer is retreating — well, there are just no words for that. Even though it means I'll be not much more than a ghost to my family on Christmas Day.

I've been working all week, which is great news for our bank account, and I've had a number of jobs confirmed for 2010, which is great. It will help us get back on our feet financially after all of this is done and dusted.

I don't have anything terribly inspiring to write this time. I've just been thinking how I'd really like to be able to kick this cancer in the nuts, like physically, for real. And then, when it's doubled over in agony, a quick knee to the face. Yep, that should do it.

I hope you all have a beautiful time this Christmas with your families and loved ones, be it white and crisp or blue skies and beaches.

And for the cancer (yes, even cancer) here's my Christmas message to you: feel free to turn it up and jump around like a madman; I am.

"Ready to Die" by Andrew W.K.

zph.com/dlt/qr2

UNTIL MY HEART CAVES IN

I've been trying to write something intelligent since Christmas Day. It hasn't really been happening. Catching my thoughts has been like Mr. Miyagi trying to catch a fly with chopsticks in *The Karate Kid*. Apparently it's known as "chemo brain" and is a well-documented occurrence. Still, it doesn't make me feel that great to know I'm not functioning 100 percent in the head. I feel a little like the crazy Irishman in *Braveheart*.

I had round six of my chemotherapy on January 4. It was supposed to be my last, but after meeting with my oncologist yesterday, it has been decided that while the treatment is working well, it should continue. So far I have had three hundred hours' worth of infusions. In two days' time, this will have increased to 350 hours as I am currently hooked up to my "takeaway" chemo—a little bottle containing a drug called 5-FU or Fluorouracil, which is mixed with a dose of folic acid. Inside the bottle is a small balloon that slowly deflates over forty-six hours, pumping the drug into my body. It's a well-established cancer treatment, about forty years old. It makes my face burn from the inside while I am connected to it. Temporary but still unpleasant. It also makes me cough a lot and burns my throat something fierce.

Combined with this, I also receive a drug called Irinotecan. All the color drains from my body while this drug goes in. I see it right before my eyes. It's quite unsettling, but I am getting used to it. It brings with it waves of exhaustion and nausea during the infusion. Apparently it has two main side effects—one being diarrhea (which I am not getting, thankfully) and the other being extreme suppression of the immune system.

This is the scary one.

When I received my first infusion, my immune system crashed. I picked up an infection from somewhere, which turned septic and left me in quite a vulnerable state. Thankfully I still had some white blood cells rolling around in my body. If not, it's quite likely I would have died. Since then, my blood cell counts have been good. Low, but within acceptable tolerances for someone being poisoned every two weeks. Funny how you can have cancer in your body but end up dying from something as simple as someone sneezing near you.

The third drug in the mix is a drug called Avastin. It is not classed as a chemical drug; it's known as a "biologic." When a tumor gets too big to feed itself via osmosis, it sends out a "request" for new blood vessels so it can tap into the bloodstream and keep feeding, keep growing. Avastin recognizes this signal and blocks it, effectively starving the tumors. The only downside I have experienced with Avastin so far is that, because it stops the creation of new blood vessels, it takes weeks for my body to heal something as basic as a paper cut.

There's a serious amount of irony involved in my being able to receive Avastin. Fact one: an old high school friend of mine works for the company that makes it. His day job is to physically manufacture the drug in the lab. Fact two: Avastin costs about $5,000 per hit. So far I've had seven of them— $35,000 worth. Thankfully the Australian government has added Avastin to the Pharmaceutical Benefits Scheme (PBS), and now it only costs me $32.50 each time. The irony? In 2008, I edited a number of videos that were used to lobby the government to have it added to the PBS, and in July 2009, three months before I was diagnosed, it was successfully added to the PBS.

Can you spell *providence*?

So each time I go into the oncology ward to have my chemo, the first thing they do besides sticking the needle into my portacath is take blood. This serves a triple purpose: one is to see if my white blood cells are high enough to cope with the treatment. If not, the treatment is halted. So far this hasn't been necessary. Two is to see if my liver is functioning OK. So far, despite the fact that on my October 6 scan my liver was covered in tumors, it is functioning perfectly. Three is to check my cancer markers—the numbers.

I live for these numbers.

I started out at 4,323 in my bloodstream and 88 in my bowel. I am now down to 750 in my bloodstream and 42.3 in my bowel. The target is less than 3 and 37, respectively.

I'm getting close.

I was a little bit disappointed that my round-five levels didn't drop further than they did, but my nurse told me they rarely get to see a patient respond the way I am responding. So given the alternative (i.e., death), I decided to keep my mouth shut and be thankful that the cancer is retreating, even if it's not as fast as I would like.

I will do whatever it takes to get well. I will fight with everything I have until my heart caves in and my body returns to the dust from which it came. I'm not giving up, no matter how weary I feel, no matter how sick I get, no matter how much it feels like I'm losing my mind, no matter how much I long for a "normal" life again. No matter what.

Until my King calls me home.

THE ACHE

The truth is ...

If I didn't have Rachel, I would let the cancer take me.

I know where I'm going when I die, so if I were alone, why wait?

Cody and Jakob are special—of course. They are an incredibly precious gift, and I love them dearly. I look at them and sometimes can't quite believe they came from me, that they're my sons and I am their father. And I would die for them—probably kill for them too, if we're being truthful.

But without Rachel, they wouldn't be here.

This treatment is starting to take its toll on me, not just physically but mentally and emotionally too—actually, mostly mentally and emotionally. Even though the cancer is dying, it is exacting a heavy price on my family and me on its way out.

Some days I'm Jekyll; some days I'm Hyde.

But mostly I'm Hyde, and I can't control it.

I feel like Charlie Gordon in the book *Flowers for Algernon* by Daniel Keyes. Charlie is a man with mental disabilities who is chosen to undergo experimental surgery to boost his intelligence. He knows he's eventually going to lose his intelligence and clarity and return to his diminished mental state. As the effects of his operation wear off, Charlie starts to see it happening before his eyes, and he knows there's nothing he can do about it. I'm not losing anything permanently, but while I'm on chemo, a few marbles have certainly escaped from the bag. It's intensely frustrating to feel it happen, and I often lash out.

I dread going to the hospital for my infusions. If you've had any form of chemotherapy, you'll understand. In my case, the six days after it are a constant fight not to vomit, not to cough myself raw, not to snap at any sound that exceeds normal everyday sound levels, not to succumb to the side effects that come from being pumped full of poison for fifty hours straight.

Chemotherapy is a generic term for any chemical treatment. In my case, more specifically, it's called cytotoxic therapy.

Cyto = cell; toxic = deadly. You do the math.

But better dread than dead, right?

God, I am aching for this to be over. My heart hurts with the knowledge of what I am putting Rachel through.

Rachel,

> *My wife. My lover. My best friend. I'm sorry you have to walk this road with me. I know you never dreamed of this when you looked at me on our wedding day and, with all of heaven watching, pledged me your love.*
>
> *Your strength is inspiring and your devotion is compelling. One day, somehow, I will make this up to you.*
>
> *I would die for you … I will live for you.*

A video Kristian made of our wedding

zph.com/dlt/qr3

MY HALLELUJAH

I've had a lot of time on my hands since Christmas. Mostly I spend it lying in bed or crashing out on the couch, mindlessly watching TV. Sometimes something good is on FOX;

other times I just channel surf to pass the time. It might sound unproductive—and prior to the cancer arriving I would have agreed—but lying in bed so often has given me the opportunity to think about a lot of things. These thoughts are the blueprints for my future. A future that is radically different from the one I envisaged five months ago.

When I was diagnosed, someone told me that after the initial shock subsided, I would get very angry. I forget who said it, but it doesn't really matter. They were wrong. As bizarre as it may sound, I feel like this cancer is quite possibly one of the best things that has ever happened to me. Yes, the treatment is horrible and my life as I knew it has been put on hold indefinitely, but it has made me reevaluate a lot of the things I once held dear. It's made me appreciate my family and friends so much more and realize that possessions mean squat when you're faced with the real possibility of dying. Most importantly, it has made me so very aware that the God I believe in is so much bigger and so much closer to me than I ever could have imagined.

Through history God has had many names, one of them being Immanuel, meaning "God with us." I have never known that to be truer than right now.

In the song "Hallelujah," Leonard Cohen sings:

There's a blaze of light in every word.
It doesn't matter which you heard
The holy or the broken hallelujah.

LEONARD COHEN, "HALLELUJAH"

I think it's safe to say that my hallelujah falls under the "broken" category.

There's little about me that would instill theologians or bishops or popes with enough confidence to pronounce it of the "holy" variety.

But that's OK with me.

I'm quite happy to be nothing and nobody. For a number of reasons, but primarily because when it's your time to stand up and do your thing and you're a nothing and a nobody, the somethings and the someones never see you coming. And there's nothing quite as effective as a blindside sucker punch.

I don't know why this cancer is here. I have to trust that God's ways are higher than my own, and whatever the reason, immense good will come from it, one way or another, and somehow this trial will become the foundation for great things done for God. Woven into the fabric of my life will be an understanding of what it is to suffer, and from that understanding will flow compassion and mercy.

Psalm 139:15–16 states this:

> *My frame was not hidden from you*
> *when I was made in the secret place,*
> *when I was woven together in the depths of the earth.*
> *Your eyes saw my unformed body;*
> *all the days ordained for me were written in your book*
> *before one of them came to be.*

So while this disease and all that comes with it may seem chaotic, I know there is method in the madness. Not my methods, but the methods of a God who holds the universe in His hands, who knew me from the moment I was conceived in the womb, who has walked beside me every day of my soon-to-be thirty-five years on this earth. I don't understand everything that's happening, and it's quite possible I never will—not while I inhabit this body anyway—but I know that whatever happens, God is in control and He has promised He will never leave me or forsake me (Hebrews 13:5).

Or, as it is translated in *The Message*:

Since God assured us, "I'll never let you down, never walk off and leave you," we can boldly quote,

God is there, ready to help;
I'm fearless no matter what.
Who or what can get to me?

I don't know about you, but that gives me a tremendous amount of confidence that everything is going to be all right. Who or what can get to me? Certainly not cancer.

Because of His goodness to me, I will sing hallelujah.

Hallelujah, because I am responding so well to treatment. So well, in fact, that my nurses can't wait to give me my blood results each time they come in.

Hallelujah, because I have a wife who loves me and who is standing with me in this battle, never flinching.

Hallelujah, because I have two beautiful, healthy children, who think their daddy is the best daddy in the world, even when his brain is messed up from the chemo drugs.

Hallelujah, because my God walks beside me and fights the battle for me. He commands His angels concerning me, and they guard me carefully. He is my fortress, my hiding place while the battle for my life rages around me. He stands between me and the sickness that seeks to take my life and says to the sickness, "No further—you will not harm him."

Hallelujah, because I am still alive and will be for many decades to come.

There are so many reasons to sing hallelujah. So many. And as long as I have air in my lungs, you will hear my hallelujah.

Whatever you see in me that you think is good comes from heaven.

It's not my doing. It's His.

HOPE LIKE FIRE

It's a good thing I'm working today. It's been a rough week so far, and the work is a welcome distraction. I think if I weren't keeping myself busy, I would probably collapse into a heap on the floor in a flood of tears. As it is, I'm finding it hard to hold it together. It's days like these that remind me this truly is a battle, and as such, some days are going to be messier than others.

I've had to deal with some (probably) well-intentioned but seriously misguided words this week. Words that have caused me deep distress and anguish. I'm OK now, but there were a few hours there where I really wanted to crack some skulls. When someone or something threatens my little family, look out. Have you ever seen a silverback gorilla detect a threat to his family? That's me—times ten.

Anyway . . .

It reads in Proverbs 18:21 (MSG):

Words kill, words give life;
   they're either poison or fruit—you choose.

As I make my way through this valley, I am becoming increasingly aware of how true that really is. The words of some people in my life are reassuring and warm. The words of others are brimming with generosity and kindness, and others speak words that still are hopeful and comforting. And there are those that are stinging with carelessness, ignorance, and doubt.

Our words are powerful. Make no mistake. They can inspire and elevate, or they can cut down and destroy. A seemingly simple comment, without consideration, can devastate, and once it's out there, you can never get it back. I used to be pretty quick with a comeback or an opinion (ask my wife), but these days, not so much. I try to consider my responses a little more carefully than I used to. It's a good thing too, because there are times when I open my mouth and I'm sure you'd really have to wonder if I truly did aspire to be like Christ when you hear what comes out.

But I'm learning—hard and fast these days.

I vividly remember driving home from the hospital the day I was diagnosed. I tried to pray, but all that came out was, "God, help." Not exactly words that inspire, but it was all I had. Even now, five months later, it's still all I've got.

There's no point in me trying to conjure up grandiose prayers in some lame attempt to be a superstar believer. This is *God* I am speaking to. If anyone can see through the smoke-screens I put up to cover my inadequacies and fears, it's Him. Thankfully, I don't have to be perfect or "holy." He's just happy for me to come, no matter how much mess I bring with me.

Chemotherapy is nothing short of drudgery. So while I'm having my infusions I've been listening to a lot of music. I really like a band called Angels & Airwaves, and have for quite a while now.

Their song "Secret Crowds" talks about words spreading hope like fire, voices that sing back louder than they were sung to.

In my most helpless moment, my voice went out in the most pathetic, desperate cry:

God, help.

And over the course of the next twenty-four hours, as word spread to our friends and family around the world, my broken, helpless voice was amplified thousands of times by those of you who took up the call to pray for me. That sound, the sound of many people gathered on my behalf, now reaches heaven not as a single, solitary voice but as a roar. And I know God has heard. He can't ignore it. It's so persistent, so consistent, so demanding, so loud that He can't help but notice and be *moved* by it.

God, help.

Those two words don't really sound like much, but they contain the two things that Jesus responded to when it came to people asking Him for healing: faith and compassion.

Faith because I have asked God for help, and in asking I expect an answer in the affirmative.

A perfect example is shown in Matthew 8:5–13 (MSG):

> *As Jesus entered the village of Capernaum, a Roman captain came up in a panic and said, "Master, my servant is sick. He can't walk. He's in terrible pain."*
> *Jesus said, "I'll come and heal him."*
> *"Oh, no," said the captain. "I don't want to put you*

to all that trouble. Just give the order and my servant will be fine. I'm a man who takes orders and gives orders. I tell one soldier, 'Go,' and he goes; to another, 'Come,' and he comes; to my slave, 'Do this,' and he does it."

Taken aback, Jesus said, "I've yet to come across this kind of simple trust in Israel, the very people who are supposed to know all about God and how he works." ...

Then Jesus turned to the captain and said, "Go. What you believed could happen has happened." At that moment his servant became well.

Compassion, because I desperately need Him to heal me, and in asking for help, I reveal my own weakness.

Matthew 20:29–34 (MSG) states this:

As they were leaving Jericho, a huge crowd followed. Suddenly they came upon two blind men sitting alongside the road. When they heard it was Jesus passing, they cried out, "Master, have mercy on us! Mercy, Son of David!" The crowd tried to hush them up, but they got all the louder, crying, "Master, have mercy on us! Mercy, Son of David!"

Jesus stopped and called over, "What do you want from me?"

They said, "Master, we want our eyes opened. We want to see!"

Deeply moved, Jesus touched their eyes. They had their sight back that very instant, and joined the procession.

He was deeply moved. Other translations say "his heart broke." What kind of God is this? That He would be deeply moved by my cry for help?

It's because I am His.

And like a father who sees his son in danger, He has come to my rescue. I hear His footsteps through the corridors of heaven. Steady and purposeful, moving toward me. The King of Kings, giving orders, commanding His angel armies to go and fight for me, to guard me carefully from my enemy, from the one who has issued this assignment on my life. The one who seeks to kill and destroy.

And the battle continues ...

I have no idea what lies ahead in the coming weeks, months—years maybe. But as much as I don't know what's coming, I do know this: there will be an end to this journey, and it will not be met with grief and sadness. It will end in triumph, and you will hear my hallelujah ringing in your ears, loud and clear, because of what *He* has done.

I'm human. My comprehension of eternal things is limited by the skin that I'm living in, but I know enough about God's character to know that His promises are rock solid. He can't lie, and He is not a man that he should change his mind.

THE DISTANCE

When I was younger, in my teens, I did a lot of concert work. Lights, sound, video—anything I could convince the people in charge I was capable of doing. It usually ended up being lights—in particular, the moving variety, as they were a new technology at the time and not many people in my town knew how to use them effectively. I talked it up a lot, but I delivered impressive results, a facet of my personality that hasn't really changed to this day.

One night in particular is still clear in my memory. It was at a church (now named Riverview) in my home town of Perth, Western Australia, and a singer named Chris Falson was there doing his thing. I'll always remember the VOX AC30 amp he played throughout that night. It was a hippie nightmare, all colorful and flowery. A custom paint job that would have looked more at home on a VW van from the 1960s than a vintage guitar amp. It was one of many shows we did around that time, but it was the night the penny dropped for me, and I knew that this was what I wanted to do with my life. For the first time ever, I saw with my eyes and heard with my ears the very same sights and sounds that played out in my heart night after night in my dreams. There was a very tangible presence of God in the room, that warm blanket I know so well, but what struck me most was the strength, the force of the delivery. Chris and the band absolutely hammered their instruments that night and showed me that you didn't have to play delicately or softly just because you were in church.

Looking back I see a lot of that night in my own guitar playing and even in my attitude toward what I do in general. At a time when a lot of people were still saying rock music didn't belong in church, Chris and his contemporaries cut their own path. When people would criticize or castigate, they would simply turn it up to eleven, set their gaze toward heaven, and keep on playing, knowing all the while that it's what they were born to do.

Eighteen years on from that night, I find one of Chris's

songs floating through my head as I lie in bed trying to sleep, night after night. In the stillness that envelops my world between 2:00 and 4:00 a.m., with the sound of the waves crashing a few hundred meters down the road at South Curl Curl Beach, the words and melody of the chorus play out, over and over.

Can you go the distance,
Make it across that line?
Or are you growing weary
Of all the people watching you?
Can you go the distance,
Make it to the end,
And write your name in glory?

CHRIS FALSON, "WIND IN HIS HAIR/
CAN YOU GO THE DISTANCE?"

After ten rounds — five months — of cytotoxic infusions, I have to tell you, I'm getting pretty weary. My body is coping remarkably well under the circumstances. I'm strong. Stronger than I ever thought I could be, but the side effects I'm experiencing, though minimal, are uncomfortable. My chemotherapy is like a carpet bombing — indiscriminate and totally destructive. Everything gets killed, even the good stuff. The term *collateral damage* has taken on a whole new meaning for me.

And I'm tired. Just really tired.

I wonder how long this season will last.

How long is the road ahead?

I know there's an end to it all somewhere, but between here and there are mountains and valleys and winding roads and corners that I can't see around. Not only do I walk the road, but my wife and children walk it too. Mentally I am always aware of their struggles in all of this, and I try to protect them from as much as I can. In guarding my own mind against fear and doubt, I'm also protecting them. I'm the head of our house, the gatekeeper. If something comes in and attacks my family, it is only because I have failed to keep it out.

More than the physical aspect of my treatment, it's the mental side that is the most tiring. Mentally I'm always on edge. I constantly think about my blood results, my CEA markers, the calendar, what day it is (I struggle to remember), when my next infusion is, how long I have been hooked up, how long I have left before disconnect. It's chaos.

And always in the back of my mind is the thought, *"What if ... ?"*

What if I don't make it?

What if I croak and let everybody down?

Some might say that's not having faith, that I shouldn't think that kind of thing. I don't know. I'm a human being, and my mortality is something that I have become acutely aware of. Ignoring the medical point of view as presented by my oncologist is not exercising faith; it's being irresponsible. Exercising faith would be trusting God's promises even when the statistics lean in cancer's favor. I tend to believe that faith is not psyching yourself up or the power of positive suggestion. I tend to see it as something far deeper and far less tangible, something not of the mind but of the soul. That place inside you that you know exists but you can't quite put your finger on. I feel like faith comes from my belly, not my head. It's something planted deep within me, and it has deep roots.

So when my humanity kicks in and I worry that maybe I won't be able to go the distance, my faith is there to reassure me that not only will I go the distance but I will do it well. I won't limp over the finish line; I will finish strong. And since my diagnosis, my faith has ruled over my humanity. A gift I sorely needed and gratefully received.

I'm not going anywhere. Cancer has been issued an eviction notice. Sure, it might protest, drag things out, appeal the ruling, but ultimately it comes down to one thing: I am not my own. I have been bought with a price. It was a heavy price, but it secured my redemption, my salvation, my life—and my health. When the soldiers drove the nails into the hands of my Savior on a hill in Jerusalem all those years ago, they weren't just hammering iron into wood, through flesh. They were nailing my cancer to that piece of wood too. That's why Jesus did it.

Isaiah 53:3–6, 10 (MSG, emphasis added) states:

> *He was looked down on and passed over,*
> *   a man who suffered, who knew pain firsthand.*
> *One look at him and people turned away.*
> *   We looked down on him, thought he was scum.*
> *But the fact is, it was* our *pains he carried—*
> *   our disfigurements, all the things wrong with us.*
> *We thought he brought it on himself,*
> *   that God was punishing him for his own failures.*
> *But it was our sins that did that to him,*
> *   that ripped and tore and crushed him—our sins!*
> *He took the punishment, and that made us whole.*
> *   Through his bruises we get healed.*

We're all like sheep who've wandered off and
gotten lost.
We've all done our own thing, gone our own way.
And God has piled all our sins, everything we've
done wrong,
on him, on him ...

Still, it's what God had in mind all along,
to crush him with pain.
The plan was that he give himself as an offering for sin
so that he'd see life come from it—life, life,
and more life.
And God's plan will deeply prosper through him.

So when this cancer stands before heaven and screams that it has a right to be here, Jesus stands up and bears witness to the fact that the cancer is mistaken and that, in fact, He took the cancer on Himself when He died and rose again, thus defeating sickness once and for all. The deal was done nearly two thousand years ago, and it can't be undone.

Revelation 1:17–18 (MSG) states:

"Don't fear: I am First, I am Last, I'm Alive. I died,
but I came to life, and my life is now forever. See these
keys in my hand? They open and lock Death's doors,
they open and lock Hell's gates."

And so it is. Cancer is finished, locked up, jailed.

That is faith.

When the doctors say it has spread from the bowel to the liver, when they say an operation is not possible yet, when my scans still show tumors present after five months of brutal treatment, I can still lift my head and say, "Yes, I see the realities of my illness. You're the mechanics, but I know the manufacturer."

Psalm 91:14–16 states:

"Because he loves me," says the LORD, *"I will*
    rescue him;
    I will protect him, for he acknowledges my name.
He will call upon me, and I will answer him;
    I will be with him in trouble,
    I will deliver him and honor him.
With long life I will satisfy him
    and show him my salvation."

I have cancer in my body but I have promises in my heart.

You will see me go the distance and you *will* see me write my name in glory. You just watch.

Not by my hand, but by His.

FROM RACHEL

There's nothing glamorous about nursing a sick spouse, nothing glamorous at all. Kristian did what he could, and he did the best he could, but he had a very short fuse during that time. We live in a little house with wooden floors, and we have two very boisterous boys, and it was not a good combination.

As much as he was trying to do the best he could, he didn't deal well with noise, especially sudden noise. I would get to the point where I had to say to him, "If you feel like your anger levels are rising, you need to go and shut yourself in the bedroom and let me deal with it." And that's often what ended up happening. Kristian could feel himself getting really agitated, and he would say, "I have to go. I have to go." And he'd just go and shut himself in the bedroom.

The downside was that the boys stopped wanting him to help them. He tried to help with bath time, but they didn't want Daddy to do anything. They wanted Mummy to get them out of the bath; they wanted Mummy to get them dressed. They became quite wary of Kristian, because they weren't sure which Daddy they were going to get. That broke him up, because he was so desperate to do what he could and to be there for them, but at times they were just not sure about him. There were times when I would meet up with my girlfriends and I'd be in tears because he'd been really angry about something. Yet he always apologized; he was so lovely like that. I knew it wasn't him; it was the medication. But it didn't make the day-to-day living any easier.

We all know somebody who's got cancer, and you see people react differently to different treatments; it's just one of those unknown things. But I wanted to know as much as I could about how I could be helpful, because I knew it was going to be up to me to keep him as comfortable as possible. I like to know what I'm up against and how things work. It was the same with cancer. I wanted to know what I was going to be in for: Is he going to be vomiting all day? Is he going to lose all his hair (the little that he had, that is)? How is this going to affect our little family?

I've never been good around sick people, and Kristian could be very trying, even when he got a cold. It was the full "man flu" experience. I was quite concerned about how I would cope if he was going to be feeling terribly sick all the time; I didn't know how much patience I would have for him.

But as soon as Kristian's condition got really serious, I simply went into full-on nurse mode. In the hospital, I would change his colostomy bag and his sheets and give him a wipedown at the end of the day. At home, I would help him in and out of the shower. We joked about him needing a bell, because when he was bedridden and he needed something, he'd have to call out to me and ask. He hated that I had to do it, but it didn't bother me at all. I was happy to do whatever I could do, because I knew it wouldn't be long. These were the times that were going to be precious because he was awake and lucid.

One of the Lucky People

DAYS LIKE THESE

April 19, 2010

I'm hanging on by a thread today.

Some days I cope quite well with all of this cancer stuff. Most days, actually. But today is not one of them.

I managed to pick up some sort of stomach bug and spent the better part of last night either sitting on, or with my head inside, the toilet. Both of which were very uncomfortable, especially the vomiting. It's like my entire stomach implodes involuntarily, like someone sucking all the air out of a paper bag. My body wants something out, and it wants it out now. It has served to remind me of exactly how vulnerable I am to even the slightest infections and how they can wreak tremendous havoc on my body.

There is no middle ground in all of this. It's either all good or all bad, and today, emotionally, I'm running on empty. I'm sitting at the table typing this, watching Jakob on the couch with his fingers in his mouth watching his favorite show, *Curious George*, and I can't help but cry. Not exactly something a man does, so they say, but I've got nothing left today. The floodgates are open. Seeing how precious my boy is only serves to reinforce how desperate this fight really is. If I don't fight, both my boys lose their daddy, and Rachel becomes a widow. That thought breaks my heart. And yet to fight is to commit myself to ongoing pain, discomfort, nausea, vomiting, burning fingers (a new drug side effect), peeling skin, and sores all over my body.

Days like today, I have no strength of my own. Though I desperately try to muster it up, I am failing miserably.

Days like these I can't help but reach out to heaven and beg for mercy.

God, help.

All I have are His promises.

> *"I'll never let you down, never walk off and leave you."*
>
> HEBREWS 13:5 MSG

God, I need a miracle, sooner rather than later. Please?

STARE THE MONSTER DOWN

Today I feel violent.

Not toward any person, but toward my cancer.

If I were on a battlefield, I would draw my sword and charge.

I will fight my enemy until I am the only one left standing. Cancer will die. I will not.

I feel it rising up on the inside of me, like a high-pressure gas pipe with nowhere to go but up and out. I can't explain it, but I know this battle is already won. The outcome is a foregone conclusion. There are angel armies lined up behind me to bring down the full force of heaven on cancer's doorstep.

Come and get some, cancer—I'm right here. It will be the last thing you ever do.

PARADOX

Making long-term plans these days is something of a luxury.

While I am convinced I will recover from this nasty little beastie called cancer, between here and there are so many uncertainties. It makes thinking ahead hard.

But I still do.

I'm making plans for all sorts of things. Holidays, music and film projects, buying a house of our own, having more children—the things you dream about when you don't have to think about whether or not you're going to die.

But as weird as it may seem, having cancer hanging over my head is something of a blessing. Why? Because I have the opportunity to learn very important things while I still have the chance to implement them and see the results enrich my life and the lives of those around me. I'm learning lessons now that most people only discover on their deathbed, and by then it's too late.

I am incredibly fortunate.

Cancer reminds me daily that my time on this earth is not, in fact, a given, and as a result, I need to live like that is indeed the case.

I don't see things the same way I used to. My physical memory is pretty much a wasteland thanks to the chemotherapy, but my heart's memory is in the best shape of my life. While I often forget day-to-day things (much to the frustration of my wife), I am constantly remembering things that are far less tangible.

I remember that I need to keep short accounts with people, because one day I may have a harsh word to say to someone and then never have the chance to apologize.

I remember that I need to be—want to be—a man of honor and integrity. Compassionate and generous. Because if I become a memory in the lives of those I love, then I want it to be a memory they cherish.

I remember that the pursuits of this world—fame, fortune, power, position, "success" (whatever that is)—are not at all important. They're just not.

And most importantly, I remember that I need to tell Rachel, Cody, and Jakob every day that I love them. Not just tell them but show them, so that if I do have to go, they will know that I really did think the world of them and that leaving them is the single biggest heartbreak I could ever imagine.

People talk of lives touched by cancer. My life wasn't "touched"; it was assaulted. I'm being held up at gunpoint, and I'm pissed about it too. But I will never let cancer see fear or intimidation in my eyes. The harder it fights me, the harder I fight back. I have everything to lose, and that fact alone makes me incredibly dangerous. So many times people associate cancer with death, and while that is the case for many people, it is not the case here. Cancer is most definitely inconvenient. It is most definitely an intrusion into our lives. It is something I would not wish on my worst enemy, but while it is here, there are good things that can be taken from it.

Genesis 50:20 (MSG) records these words:

"Don't you see, you planned evil against me but God used those same plans for my good, as you see all around you right now—life for many people."

I have an opportunity in front of me that most people rarely get. I have the opportunity to reclaim life from a place where there is usually death.

That makes me one of the luckiest people on the planet.

TICKTOCK

This morning I went up to the hospital for my (now) tri-weekly blood tests and to pick up my next round of eighty-four chemo tablets. The tablets last fourteen days, and after that, I have a week off in order to give my immune system a chance to recover. I go early in the morning, and it's usually quiet in oncology at that time of day. But today was quite busy, so I waited around for a bit while the nurses tended to other patients who were getting infusions.

Some of the faces there are becoming quite familiar, and we seem to have an unspoken understanding of what each other has been through, and more importantly, what is still to come.

Today there were two new faces. One lady who looked like cancer was getting the better of her, and she knew it too. It was easy to see the fear in her eyes, and I felt like I should go over to her and hug her. But of course that would be inappropriate, especially considering we don't know each other. So I just smiled at her each time she looked at me.

The other new face wasn't a patient at all, but rather the wife of a patient. She came in just as I was about to leave, her eyes red and tears running down her face. The nurses met her in the corridor and they all hugged her and cried softly together. Cancer had taken her husband during the night, and she had come over to inform the nurses and thank them for all they had done to help him.

I sat there choking back tears myself. I knew exactly what this woman was going through, and there was nothing I could do to help her. Death had visited her house, and there was nothing anyone could do.

My nurses said their good-byes and then both quietly slipped into their office to compose themselves before attending to the rest of the waiting patients. I sat there, still, quiet. Not knowing if I should speak or just quietly slip out.

In the end I went to their office, signed my paperwork quietly, and left.

I am struggling to process what I saw today. I am struggling to reconcile the fact that I am getting better while other people are dying.

Why me?

Why them?

Why cancer at all?

I was speaking with my oncologist recently, and he was deeply offended when I told him there were some people who were asking about my prognosis. He was of the opinion that it was a most invasive question to ask and that they really had no right to ask such a thing at all. He was very defensive and told me that if anyone asks again, I should tell them my prognosis is certain death, just like everyone else on the planet.

I thought about this as I walked out of the hospital, still very upset, and as I walked down the service road toward my car, I started to speak to God. Because, really, when it comes to life and death, who else do you speak to?

God, You can stop this. Why don't You?

Silence.

It's not for me to know.

In Isaiah 55:8 (MSG), God tells us:

"I don't think the way you think.
The way you work isn't the way I work.
For as the sky soars high above earth,
so the way I work surpasses the way you work,
and the way I think is beyond the way you think."

While I firmly believe that life itself is truly a gift, I am also very aware that there is appointed to us all a time to live and a time to die. That's the way of things, and they are well and truly out of my control.

Still. I don't like the idea of dying.

The British comedian Lenny Henry once said that he felt it would be much more polite for Death to make an appointment before coming to see you, like the gas man or the plumber. A little note slipped under your front door — "Sorry I missed you today. I will be back for you tomorrow at 3:30."

At least then you could be out.

PRECIOUS METAL

June 9, 2003: that's the day Rachel and I were married. Seven years ago today.

It was a Monday, a public holiday, and we decided it would be cool if we got married at dusk. So I set the start time on our invitations at 4:44 p.m. So many people asked why on earth I picked that time, and I was only too happy to tell them that I wanted people to remember the time and *be* on time. The fact that they were talking about it meant they were much less likely to forget it. And besides, it was my wedding, and I could have it start at whatever time I felt like.

An hour or so after my funny little starting time, Rachel and I were husband and wife. On her finger was a white-gold ring that sat nicely next to her engagement ring, and on mine was a similar ring. Our jeweler had informed us that while most people used nickel as the base for their white-gold rings, he proudly used platinum. It wasn't something I had given much thought to when it came to having our rings made, but I knew enough to know that platinum is a whole lot more valuable than nickel, and as it was going to be given to my bride, this precious metal was most fitting.

Seven years, and I can guarantee that when we both promised to stick it out "in sickness and in health," neither of us imagined anything like what we're going through now.

In three days, I will be dealing with platinum once again. Only this time it will be going *into* my body and not on it.

Over the past three weeks, the numbers that show how active the cancer is in my body—my CEA markers—have increased. They have moved from their lowest point at 258 to 504. This isn't a large increase considering I started at 4,323 (a normal person is 3 or less) but as a percentage, they have doubled. So it's been decided that in conjunction with the Xeloda tablets I am taking, I will also head back to the hospital for a further round of infusions. This time it will be a drug named Oxaliplatin given every three weeks. According to Wikipedia, Oxaliplatin "features a square planar platinum(II) centre. In contrast to cisplatin and carboplatin, Oxaliplatin features the bidentate ligand 1,2-diaminocyclohexane in place of the two monodentate ammine ligands. It also features a bidentate oxalate group."

Umm … right. OK. If you understand any of that, then give yourself a pat on the back, because I don't. I just know that they're going to push platinum into my bloodstream and somehow it's going to pick a fight with my cancer.

My previous regimen consisted of three drugs in conjunction with folic acid, a mixture that proved very effective but one that also wiped me out for a week at a time. This new regimen is designed to maintain the ground we have taken until I finish working on a TV series, after which I will go back to the original regimen with the view to having surgery in a few months' time to forcibly remove the tumors in my liver. Apparently it's quite possible to remove up to three-quarters of the human liver, and in six to eight weeks it will grow back, healthy and cancer free. It's the only organ in the body that has that ability, a superpower of sorts.

So we're going into another holding pattern while I earn enough money to see us through the recovery period—and beyond if necessary.

When I first started chemo, I really had no idea what to expect. I was so naive that I even booked (and showed up to) work on the two days immediately following that first infusion. Of course, my body was in total shock after its first taste of poison and I crashed—hard. This time, I have spent some time researching my next round of poison, and to be honest, I'm more than a little anxious.

You see, Oxaliplatin affects nerve ends as a side effect. Primarily, this will manifest itself as an extreme sensitivity to the cold, which is wonderful as we head into winter. Along with the usual suspects like nausea, vomiting, and diarrhea, there is another, more worrisome side effect.

Hearing loss.

It's nowhere near as common as the previously mentioned side effects, but it's the one that scares me the most.

I make my living with my ears—as an editor, as a sound engineer, as a musician. It's all I've known since I graduated from high school, and to be honest, I love what I do.

But I'm nervous. Really nervous. Please pray that this side effect does not come knocking on my door.

I still struggle to understand all that is happening in my life, in our lives as a family. It's quite likely that I never will fully grasp it all. But one thing I do know is that it takes incredible pressure, from all sides, to turn a lump of coal into a diamond. I think it's fair to say I'm being squeezed pretty hard right now; Rachel too. But when this is all over and the transformation is complete, the light reflected by my life, our lives, will be something to behold, and you will know where that light comes from.

There will be no doubt.

Happy anniversary, babe. I love you.

BRICK BY BRICK

I went into the hospital today for another blood test. The one they do before I start my tablets to make sure my white blood cell count is strong enough to deal with the chemo. I had one done four days ago too, to make sure I was OK to take the Oxaliplatin infusion. The results from that blood test came back this morning. My cancer markers have increased again, from 504 to 674.

So far the last four blood tests have gone like this: 258 → 340 → 504 → 674.

That's an increase of 161 percent.

This is what's known as a "trend." And my cancer markers are trending up—which means the cancer is active again.

Sigh. Here we go again.

I'm trying to remember what God has promised me about my future, but all I can see right now is the number 674 flashing like a Don't Walk sign. I am feeling very human—very vulnerable, very fragile, and very much mortal. All the work that's been done so far, all that's been achieved, nine months of hell on my body—it's all going backward right now. But that's why my doc put me on the Oxaliplatin, I guess. He saw it coming.

Apparently it's a pretty mean cancer drug. A friend who has a similar diagnosis to mine told me it was the single worst chemo drug he's been on. I guess in that respect I'm being looked after, because I'm actually feeling fine physically. A little seedy at times, but nothing an antinausea pill can't fix. I have been working since the day after the infusion, and apart from feeling really tired—like, *really* tired—I seem to be handling it quite well. The neuropathy that comes with it is manageable as long as I take precautions against the cold.

But I can't help feeling cheated. We worked so hard to get to 258 from 4,323.

Five hundred hours of IV infusions. Days laid up in bed, desperately fighting the nausea and other side effects, and now it feels like it's slipping away.

I'm sure it will be temporary, but the feeling of being robbed is still very strong. I'm getting angry, because I feel this is a gross injustice. I don't get angry at a lot of things, but injustice is most definitely my main trigger, and right now I'm livid. Were cancer a physical being, were it human and right in front of me, I would have no hesitation snapping its neck. And I'd sleep with a clear conscience afterward too.

Sorry if this isn't what you've come to expect from me. I'm really struggling today. But it will lift, even if we have to build it back one CEA marker at a time.

At least I have some new music from Train to lift me up. I'm really looking forward to seeing them in concert next week. Funny how we often expect God to work through "godly" things. Things or people that are "holy" or "blessed." I don't know about the guys from Train and where they stand with the Big Guy, but right now I'm drawing courage from their music, and that's fine with me. It's good medicine.

GOD, HELP

My cancer markers have doubled again. Blood results from three days ago.

This is not good.

Rachel is in New Zealand with the boys, spending some time with her family, and I can't get in contact with her.

I'm a mess. Our house is empty save for the sound of my sobbing, and it's cold, which means the neuropathy is very painful right now.

God, help.

If You don't, I'm dead.

THE WEIGHT

I'm tired. Worn-out.

Not just physically but emotionally. This disease is sitting heavy on my body and on my spirit, and the weight is getting me down. It's been nine months now, but yesterday was the worst single day for me since I was diagnosed. Cancer markers rising; I couldn't contact Rachel. I felt incredibly isolated and helpless.

Realistically, there is absolutely nothing I can do to make myself better. Not a thing. It's completely out of my hands, like so much of our lives these days. Everything is "wait and see." My life is now not mine in the most literal sense possible. All I can do is keep asking God to intervene and keep showing up for chemo, which is kind of daunting, given what it does to my body.

Yesterday I was pretty frightened, and I found myself uttering those familiar words — *God, help* — though this time with a renewed sense of urgency.

It's one thing to believe that God is going to do something when the picture is fine and dandy and the cancer levels are decreasing. It's another thing entirely when the cancer levels are going up with such regularity. This is where faith really comes into its own. The Bible defines faith as "the substance of things hoped for, the evidence of things not seen." My recovery, my healing, most certainly fits those two characteristics. Right now it is very much hoped for and very much unseen, at least to the human eye.

It would be really easy to get pissed off at God for a whole host of reasons. Let's start with having cancer in the first place and move on from there. But God didn't give me this disease. As I have said before, He's not that kind of God. Spiteful vengeance and retaliatory payback are not in His nature. It's impossible for those things to be present in a being who is called Love (1 John 4:8). So by working out what God *is*, it's easy to deduce what He *isn't*. And He isn't the kind of guy who goes around hitting people up with terminal diseases.

But why then is this disease even here at all? I have no family history of cancer. I am—for the most part—healthy (though Rachel would argue I don't get nearly enough exercise); I don't drink or do drugs (never have) and live a pretty clean lifestyle.

So why is it here?

I have no idea.

And I really wish that it wasn't something I had to contend with.

I wish that the word *oncology* were a word that was rarely, if ever, present in my vocabulary.

I wish that I had no idea what a CEA marker count was.

I wish that every little pop, cramp, and twinge in my body didn't make me stop and wonder what was going on.

I wish that Cody didn't try to identify with me by having

"a sore stomach like you, Dad," even when he doesn't have a sore stomach. As beautiful as it is that he wants to be like his daddy, how painful it is for me that he is trying to emulate cancer symptoms in order to do so. Bless his little heart. I'm so glad he doesn't understand what is really going on. One day I will sit him down and explain all of this to him. I'll tell him how Daddy was very scared that he would have to leave him and not be able to come back and that Daddy fought very hard to make sure he got to stay around. I'll show him the photos, the doctors' reports, the scans and X-rays, the scars, so he will know what great lengths I went to so that I would be there for him. He will know how much I love him by what I endured for him.

And he will know how God rescued his daddy.

One day.

But in the meantime, it's one foot in front of the other. Day by day, sometimes minute by minute. Just keep swimming.

Second Corinthians 12:7–10 (MSG) states this:

> Satan's angel did his best to get me down; what he in fact did was push me to my knees. No danger then of walking around high and mighty! At first I didn't think of it as a gift, and begged God to remove it ... and then he told me,
>
> > My grace is enough; it's all you need.
> > My strength comes into its own in your weakness.

And so the weaker I get, the stronger I become.

That's the paradox, the contradiction of God. My weakness makes room for His strength. In these times that are fearful and tiring and uncertain, when I feel I have nothing left in the tank, God shows up and reminds me that there is indeed nothing I can do. And He offers me His strength, because it is more than enough to carry this weight.

Do I understand it?

Of course not.

Do I believe it?

With every fiber of my being. And I will hold on to it until my last breath.

ODYSSEY

I'd been putting it off all day. I needed to call the oncology ward and find out my latest blood test results, but I was, quite frankly, afraid to do so after the last few weeks of increased cancer activity (as evidenced by the rise in my CEA markers). I know putting it off achieves nothing. The results will be what they will be, and delaying the phone call to find out makes no difference. But when you're dealing with issues of life and death—your own life and death—sometimes you look for any way of delaying what might possibly be bad news.

I slept most of the day (as I did for most of Saturday and Sunday too) and by 4:00 p.m. figured I should stop putting it off. So I rang.

I spoke to one of my nurses, and she told me she was just about to call me with the results. There was a split second where I couldn't tell whether the news was going to be good or bad. I feel like I know my nurses pretty well by now, after ten months of chemo, but interpreting their tone of voice is not always easy. Especially if they're busy at the time. There's a lot of checking and rechecking involved in administering cytotoxic drugs. Patient ID numbers must be checked against the date of birth, which must be checked against Medicare numbers, etc., etc. Once the written checks are done, the verbal ones begin. Name? Date of birth? Needle size? They get very busy and have to maintain intense concentration levels, so sometimes it's hard to figure out which way the news is going to go.

Thankfully, my nurse followed it up with, "I think I'm going to make your day."

Relief.

But how much? That's always the question.

As it turns out, my cancer markers have decreased 10 percent since last week, without another infusion in between.

This is good news. It means that the drugs are taking control of the cancer again. Granted they're the heavy-duty kind of drugs that really mess me up. The ones that make me feel like a hollow shell. The ones that make it difficult to move without waves of nausea. The ones that make me incredibly sensitive to the cold. The ones that turn me from Jekyll to Hyde ... but they're working.

So I won't complain. Even though I'm just so tired of feeling this way, both physically and emotionally, there is an awful lot to be thankful for.

And that's the thing. Through all of this — crap — that cancer brings with it and for all the damage it does to my body, my mind, my intellect, there is still gold that can be found along the way.

A good friend of mine recently described this as not a journey or an experience, but as an odyssey.

Odyssey is defined in the *Macmillan Dictionary* as "a long journey during which many things happen" or "a person's progress from one stage of life or set of beliefs to another."

My friend was right.

There is nothing simple about this ride. No easy trip from point A to point B. It is, without a doubt, the hardest thing I have ever had to endure in my thirty-five years on this earth. And even though I'm young and strong, it's still hard—and I long for the day it is over.

The day my odyssey ends.

The day my doctor looks at me with a hint of disbelief and tells me there is no evidence of disease in my body.

The day I see with my eyes what I already see with my heart.

Thankfully, there is someone who has already walked this road before me, someone who was "familiar with pain" (Isaiah 53:3) and acquainted with sorrow.

I can't see what's up ahead, though I desperately look for any kind of sign. So I keep my head down, focusing on the footprints of Him who has gone before me.

Though the way is rough and steep, it is the path to the One I seek. I must go on.

I'll follow in the path of the man with the nail scars in his hands.

DAVID MEECE, "THE MAN WITH THE NAIL SCARS"

PROMISES—PART 1

Chemotherapy: round fourteen.

The house is empty. Rachel and the boys are at a birthday

party for one of Cody's little friends. It's both a blessing and a curse.

A blessing because the house is quiet and I can get some rest and let the nausea and other side effects pass me by.

A curse because I so love Rach and the boys, and I love their company.

I love watching the boys as they potter around the house playing with their toys, watching TV, bouncing on the trampoline, or playing with Daisy, our kitten. Watching Cody be the "boss" and seeing Jakob watch everything Cody does and so want to be like him. The big brother/little brother dynamic. The older they get, the more their personalities emerge, and it is truly a beautiful thing to witness.

I have the next week off. Chemotherapy is as good an excuse as any to take it easy for a few days. I've been struggling a lot with the pressure in my work life and am looking for ways to minimize it, as it is starting to affect me negatively. I'm struggling mentally in quite a few areas these days. Memory, perception of reality, emotional control—it's starting to pile up, and it's getting harder to stay on the Jekyll side of things. More and more I see myself leaning to the Hyde side, and it's distressing, as it feels as though I am heading out of control. So as much as I hate to admit it, I've taken some sage advice and am going to see a psychologist over the coming weeks. My mental health is just as important as my physical health, so I need to do something about it.

On top of that, my body is weak, and I'm constantly tired to the point of exhaustion.

So I'm flicking through the TV guide on FOX and looking for something to pass the time, when I hear a familiar voice and sound. It's Peter Furler, former Newsboys lead singer. I generally avoid the Christian channel on TV, as I find it less than excellent in many areas, but Peter's voice makes me stop. The band is playing underneath him and he's reciting Scripture, but not parrot-fashion. He believes what he's saying, and that makes his words, the words of God, powerful. They cut through the chemo haze and go straight to my heart.

So do not fear, for I am with you;
  do not be dismayed, for I am your God.
I will strengthen you and help you;
  I will uphold you with my righteous right hand.

All who rage against you
  will surely be ashamed and disgraced;
those who oppose you
  will be as nothing and perish.
Though you search for your enemies,
  you will not find them.
Those who wage war against you
  will be as nothing at all.
For I am the LORD your God
  who takes hold of your right hand
and says to you, Do not fear;
  I will help you.

ISAIAH 41:10 – 13

And then peace floods the room and the tears fall again — grateful tears. My God has promised to look after me, to bring help. My God, who defends me, who is far greater in strength than my cancer or any fear that comes because of it. My God, who spoke and whose words caused the universe to be.

His word is true, unfailing. If He promises something, He will deliver.

I'd stake my life on it.

PROMISES—PART 2

I just got my blood test results back. They're not good. They're not bad either, I suppose. I'm still responding to the treatment, which is good—just not like I once was. Without speaking to my oncologist, I can't really explain it to you as I don't understand it myself. One set of markers has come down by 2 percent while the other has gone up by 40 percent. And of course, this is all on different drugs from what I was on previously.

It seems everywhere I turn, though, there is encouragement. While my humanity would have me believe there is much wrong with my current situation (and believe me, it is becoming harder and harder to fight my humanity), it would appear that God Himself has set up a series of "road signs" to keep me going in the right direction. When it would be very easy for me to lose my way, to become blinded by circumstance, He has gone before me and left His own "markers" to make sure I keep going. The right words at the right time do not speak of coincidence to me. They speak of planning, timing, design—and my God is the master designer. Take a look outside your window one day at sunset. Tell me a master artist isn't at work in that moment.

I have a friend who, in my opinion, is one of the finest

examples of the word *gentleman* I have ever met. His intellect is only surpassed by the size of his heart and his ability to show compassion.

He has gently reminded me that even though this walk is frightening, lonely and unsure (from a human perspective), when Christ entered this world as flesh and blood He came with the name Immanuel.

Matthew 1:23 states:

The virgin will conceive and give birth to a son, and they will call him Immanuel (which means, "God with us").

Christ came to be God with us, entering into our situation with us so that we'd know we're never alone, no matter the circumstances.

I have pain in my liver most days. The tumors on the liver press against my abdomen and cause a stitch-like feeling. The abdomen then presses against a nerve that runs up the right side of my body, which shows itself as an aching right shoulder. While I have a constant reminder in my body that there is something that would seek to destroy me and take me away from my wife and children, I also have a constant reminder that God Himself walked this earth as a man. He knows pain. He understands sorrow, and He knows what it is to face death.

Without wanting to sound melodramatic, so do I.

But His name promises me that He is here, with me.

Every time I call out, I call out that promise, reminding myself.

FROM RACHEL

Our wedding day was simply a really fun day. Even though we had such a memorable start time, the ceremony ended up being a little bit late because a friend of mine with a carload of Kiwis got lost and we waited for them to arrive. That meant that it got a bit darker, so the candles in the church were even more spectacular. The reception was so much fun, just how we wanted it; we're not dancers, so we didn't have a dance floor and we didn't have a deejay. We just wanted good food and good company. I felt beautiful, as you're supposed to feel on your wedding day, and it was really fun. Everything went so smoothly because Kristian had done a lot of the planning; he loved that sort of thing, and that was fine by me.

Even though Kristian was such a planner, I'd say his proposal was a fairly standard one. You hear some stories of other people's proposals being quite remarkable, and he was perhaps a bit disappointed that he didn't do something spectacular. He said to me afterward, "Oh, was mine all right?"

I knew it was coming; even so, he did surprise me. We'd already been to a jeweler, and I'd picked out what sort of ring I wanted, and we'd decided we were having a night wedding. One evening, we went into the city to check out some locations for the wedding photos. I think Kristian's plan was to propose on the steps of the Opera House, but we ended up walking around to The Rocks. There was a beautiful spot that looked out across to the Harbour Bridge, and that's where he pulled out the ring and proposed. He didn't go down on one knee, which was fine because I'm not into that, and I'm so glad he didn't do it in a restaurant because that's just not me either. It wasn't flamboyant, but it was beautiful.

In the early days when Kristian started his treatment, going back to New Zealand was necessary for me on a number of levels. I needed a break, and he knew that. He knew it was hard for me, that I needed to go home and get loved on and get my tank filled up again. But he hated it when we were gone. That first time we went without him, I thought it would be a relief for Kristian because the house would be quiet and he could just rest. But he hated it; even though we'd Skype every day and talk on the phone a few times a day, he missed us so much.

I always felt a bit guilty because I missed him, but at the same time I didn't—I just needed the break. It was a very necessary time to get my batteries recharged and for the boys to see their cousins and their nanna and poppa. They always had a great time when we went to New Zealand, and that was important for them as well. It was good to come home, though, because I was ready to come back and keep going.

Soon after announcing our engagement

Wonderful Inconvenience

DAYS THAT MATTER

Today is Rachel's birthday.

She's heading out the door to church with the boys, and I'm staying at home, supposedly to do some housework and also because it's only been a week since chemo and I'm (cough, cough) not feeling too good (cough, cough).

Truth be told, the last four weeks I've been on a marathon planning crusade to organize a surprise party as well as a few other bits and pieces. Rachel is a very social creature, not like me at all in that regard, and thrives on the company of her friends. While a good number of them can't be here for the surprise due to the fact they live in New Zealand, there's enough people who love her on their way to make it worthwhile. She doesn't know it yet, but in three hours there's going to be twenty-five adults and kids running around, playing on a cool little bouncy castle, eating fully catered food all served to them by waitstaff, a selection of imported beers (don't worry, I don't drink), and of course, excellent New Zealand wines to toast the birthday girl.

I've got to go and organize the last few little things. In the meantime, here's a video I made for Rachel as a birthday

present. Kiwi people, keep an eye out for a special guest—
and some guy who calls himself Wolverine.

Rachel's birthday video

zph.com/dlt/qr4

OVERWHELMED

The past week has been like nothing I have ever experienced.

The only thing I can liken this to is a tsunami of care and kind words from people I have never met from all over the planet. A lot of you don't even speak my language. (Thank goodness for online translators!) Nonetheless, you have taken the time to comment or send an email in response to Rachel's birthday video, and in all honesty, most of you have had me in tears. Such kindness from total strangers.

I only ever put Rachel's video on the Web in order to share it with our friends and family. Many of them live so far away, and I wanted them to be able to share in Rachel's birthday in some small way. But then it got a little crazy, and … well … here we are.

I have no words to thank you for your support. I'm really at a loss.

Please know that from here on out, the encouragement you have all sent is going to be sorely needed. Things look like they are going to get a lot worse before they start to get better. I'm sorry.

Please keep me in your prayers. Rachel and the boys too. We're going to need every ounce of strength we can find in the coming months.

I WISH ...

Yesterday I went back in for new CT scans. It's been five months since my last set of scans were done, and the surgeon who is looking after me ordered something more current. I don't know the results of these scans yet, but based on the last set of scans, it's not possible to operate on my liver due to the placement of the tumors. Something about "bilateral metastasis."

On top of that, my CEA and CA markers from my most recent blood test have come back 50 percent higher again. My CEAs have come in around 1,500, and my CAs have come back at 75. For anyone who understands these numbers, you will know that these figures are high and not a good sign. It's not necessarily an indicator of aggression from the cancer, but it does show tumor activity—multiplication and division. I guess one good sign is that all blood tests show healthy and normal liver function. Surprising to me, but welcome, very welcome.

When I finally got home from the hospital, I was wasted. Physically: drained, nauseated, and sleepy. Emotionally: empty, unsure, and afraid.

I want so desperately for this journey to end.

I want my life back.

Cancer has taken so much from us this past year. I want it back. All of it.

God? Please?

If it be your will,
if there is a choice,
let the rivers fill,
let the hills rejoice.
Let your mercy spill
on all these burning hearts in hell
if it be your will
to make us well.

And draw us near
and bind us tight,
all your children here
in their rags of light.
In our rags of light,
all dressed to kill
and end this night.

If it be your will.

LEONARD COHEN, "IF IT BE YOUR WILL"

I wish for a body free of disease.

I wish for the chance to have another child with Rachel.

I wish for the chance to comfort my boys when they get their hearts broken by a girl for the first time.

I wish for the chance to take them to their first U2 concert.

I wish for the chance to see them become men, to tell them how my heart swells with pride when I see what they have become.

I wish for the chance to hold Rachel's hand, to offer her my arm, to steady her in her old age. To tell her she's still beautiful when a lifetime of smiles are visible on her face.

I wish I understood why I have cancer.

I wish for many things, but most of all I wish for life.

LEARNING TO FLY

I'm not feeling too good right now.

I'm making my way through round sixteen of chemotherapy, and so far it's been pretty awful.

The last few months I have been receiving treatments every three weeks. This was for an infusion and then two weeks' worth of Xeloda tablets. As my CEA and CA markers are still climbing, it's been decided I should go off the Xeloda and back to the 5-FU infusion. Which is good; it's what I wanted. Only problem is that the Xeloda hasn't had the extra week it usually has to get itself out of my system. That, coupled with the heavy dose of 5-FU, means that yesterday and today have brought some of the most intense pain in my hands and feet I have ever experienced. My hands and feet burn; I walk like an old man shuffling down the hall. I can't hold anything in my hands, and my feet and hands are purple. I can't do anything to ease the burning sensation, as I am also receiving the drug Oxaliplatin, the main side effect of which is an extreme sensitivity to the cold. This means I get quite painful pins and needles whenever I'm exposed to the cold. On the one hand, my body is burning, and on the other, I can't use anything cold to try to relieve it. So I have to ride it out.

On top of all that, my CA 19-9 markers have come back in at 87.9. I started chemotherapy almost a year ago, and they were at 88. It feels like I have been through hell for nearly twelve months, and now I'm right back where I was at the beginning and I have to do it all over again. I'm devastated.

It's been a pretty rough forty-eight hours.

But...

Jakob turned two the other week, and I was here to see it.

It was so much fun watching his little face light up as he opened each new present. He is just learning to talk, so most of his communication comes in the form of sounds that sound like words but aren't quite there yet. As much as I want him to start talking so we can communicate better, a part of me wishes he would stay an unintelligible little chatterbox for as long as possible. It does my heart good to listen to him chatter away.

Cody and Jakob are two very different people. Cody is very much an alpha male. Wherever we go, Cody usually ends up with a bunch of kids following him and doing whatever he suggests; he's like the Pied Piper. Jakob, on the other hand, is a comedian in training. When he gets a positive reaction to his antics, he repeats them at will as long as the laughter continues—or until he gets bored. I must say, it's very hard to resist his cheeky little grin.

I love them both so much.

Whenever I come home from work or the hospital, both Cody and Jakob run down the hallway to meet me. It's a moment I look forward to from the moment I leave the house, especially when I'm heading up to the hospital for another round of chemotherapy. Over the last few months I have noticed that when Jakob greets me, a good portion of his approach is flat-out running, but at the very last minute, he launches himself into the air and it's up to me to catch him.

I don't think it has ever occurred to him that I *won't* catch him. He trusts me completely.

And that's where I'm at right now—running as best I can and hurling myself into the arms of my heavenly Father.

Trusting that He will not let me fall.

Trusting that, despite the rising cancer markers in my body, I am very much on His radar and that what I am going through is known to (and understood by) Him.

Trusting that He is a God who heals. A God who is full of mercy and compassion.

A God who is with me as I walk through this seemingly endless valley.

IF NOT FOR LOVE

Our world fell down around us one year ago today: Diagnosis Day.

Fast-forward one year to the day, and I am heading up to the hospital for my seventeenth chemo infusion. The irony is not lost on me.

It's hard to know whether to celebrate because I have made it through the year or to be despondent because I have been living with this disease and going through chemo for a year with little in the way of medical results to show for it.

We would have been just about to have our third child now, but that's off the table for the foreseeable future. It's an ache I feel deep inside me as I see Rachel put on her bravest face, though I know inside her mother's heart is breaking.

So much stolen from us, so much.

Because of me. Because *my* body is broken.

All our plans lie scattered on the ground like someone has opened a window and sent a pile of papers flying through the air. Our future is as easy to pin down as a mosquito buzzing around your ear in the middle of the night.

Because of me.

God, save us. Save our family. Restore what has been taken from us, with interest for all the crap we've had to endure.

I know Your arm is not too short that it can't reach out and put an end to this madness.

I know You can.

Because through it all—through the burning skin, the vomiting, the nausea, the exhaustion, the nosebleeds, the ulcers, the pins and needles, the peeling skin, the mood swings, the rising markers—I hear the still, small voice of Your Spirit, leading me on. Gently urging me forward.

When tomorrow has been stolen, and you can't
*   lift your head,*
And summer feels like winter, your heart is
*   full of stone.*
Though all your hopes have fallen, your skin is now
*   your only armor*
Wear your scars like medals, defender of the faith.

Come, come lay your weary head. Be still my friend.
Come, rise. I'll place my sword upon your shoulder.

Come, come lay your faithful head. Be still
  my friend.
Come. Rise with me.

  DELIRIOUS?, "WHEN ALL AROUND HAS FALLEN"

If not for Love, Love that laid down His own life in place of mine, how would I make it through this? I know I am overshadowed by the biggest set of wings ever seen. I look up and know I am covered. I know I will be safe, protected, though I don't know in what form that safety will arrive—or when.

In Psalm 91:1–12 (MSG) God promises this:

You who sit down in the High God's presence,
  spend the night in Shaddai's shadow,
Say this: "GOD, you're my refuge.
  I trust in you and I'm safe!"
That's right—he rescues you from hidden traps,
  shields you from deadly hazards.
His huge outstretched arms protect you—
  under them you're perfectly safe;
  his arms fend off all harm.
Fear nothing—not wild wolves in the night,
  not flying arrows in the day,
Not disease that prowls through the darkness,
  not disaster that erupts at high noon.
Even though others succumb all around,
  drop like flies right and left,
  no harm will even graze you.
You'll stand untouched, watch it all from a distance . . .

Yes, because GOD's your refuge,
    the High God your very own home,
Evil can't get close to you,
    harm can't get through the door.
He ordered his angels
    to guard you wherever you go.
If you stumble, they'll catch you;
    their job is to keep you from falling.

Like I said, I don't know how it will arrive or when, but I know this: it's coming.

You wait and see.

SIRT—PART 1

Tomorrow morning at 7:30 a.m., I am to present myself to St. Vincent's Hospital for tests to determine whether or not I am able to receive SIRT. That's short for Selective Internal Radiation Therapy.

It's pretty intense. They're going to inject thousands of tiny radioactive particles directly into my liver in an attempt to kill the tumors. It is usually very successful, but it's heavy-duty, and if it goes ahead, I will be flat on my back for about four weeks afterward.

I've already met with the surgeon responsible for the procedure, and tomorrow they'll give me an angiogram, a CT scan, and then, as I understand it, insert one radioactive sphere (a SIR-Sphere). This is all designed to track how the blood and radiation flow through my liver.

In a perfect world, there will be no leakage from my liver into the bowel or lungs or through the hepatic artery as this can cause complications further down the line. Doc says 85 percent of people respond well to this treatment, which is to say that only 15 percent don't. Medically speaking, these are the best odds I've been given so far.

If you pray, now would be a good time. This is by far the scariest procedure I've encountered so far. Even though chemo makes me feel awful, I know what to expect when it comes. This treatment is a completely unknown element for me, and I'm a little anxious. Anxious that it might burn; anxious that I might not be able to receive the full-scale radiation infusion due to the way my body is wired; anxious that there will be a fair degree of poking and prodding all day long and a decent level of discomfort for the duration. And of course, the needles. I don't like needles.

I'm going to be carrying this picture with me, to remind myself what it's all for, should the fear begin to creep in.

I'll do anything to defend this.

SIRT – PART 2

So today was the "trial run" of the SIR-Sphere insertion.

It was awful, but it worked. My body is doing exactly what the doctors want it to, and so after hours of poking, prodding, endless contrast injections, and general discomfort, the green light is given. I'm home and in a bit of pain, but the treatment will be possible.

I go in for the real deal on Wednesday, November 3.

Today I had an angiogram where I got to see all the blood vessels in my liver in action. Then I had a CT scan, and then I went down to the nuclear medicine department and was photographed endlessly by a gamma camera. All very high-tech and expensive. Glad the technology exists or I'd be toast, medically speaking.

But thinking ahead, I'm more than a little anxious, now that I know what I will be facing again. The insertion of the catheter into my groin was less than thrilling, and once again, my dignity was blown away as anyone and everyone who was working on me was subjected to my private bits each time they wanted to do anything. Such a wonderful feeling, to dress up in their gowns only to have them immediately cut off once I'm lying on the table. But the potential benefits far outweigh the drawbacks, so I just need to man up and get on with it.

Being in all these specialized treatment rooms today made me so aware, again, of how serious all of this stuff really is and so appreciative of our Medicare and hospital systems. The staff at St. Vincent's Hospital was overwhelmingly comforting and kind. They were totally professional and really deserve far more recognition than they currently receive. One of the guys working on me during the angiogram, David, has had prostate cancer himself. His words were so comforting, as I knew that he knew exactly what was going on inside my head. He was able to make me laugh over and over as the day continued. That kind of empathetic knowledge is priceless.

On top of that, I was tended to in the recovery ward by a beautiful man named Peter. He would check up on me regularly, offering food or drinks. He would hold the cup while I drank, as I was not allowed to sit upright or move at all for three hours. Then he would go around to the other patients and do the same thing for them. As it turns out, he does this work voluntarily—no pay. I think when I get clear of all of this cancer stuff, I need to take a page out of Peter's book. A kind word or the simple act of holding a cup can be the difference between a good day and a really bad day for some people. Especially when fear is knocking loudly on the door, as it so often does in hospital situations.

The SIR treatment is quite a bit more expensive than we were first told: $7,000 instead of $5,000. The procedure itself is covered by the Australian government's Medicare system, but the radioactive spheres are not. But thanks to the generosity of a number of audio engineers and musicians around Australia, we don't have to find too much extra cash to get it underway. They donated just over the $5,000 mark within a week—yet 95 percent of them have never met me. Once again I was astounded and humbled. Just days earlier, I had specifically asked God for a way to afford this treatment. The guys who donated didn't know that, but God moved in their hearts anyway.

Philippians 4:19 (MSG) states:

*You can be sure that God will take care of everything
you need, his generosity exceeding even yours in the
glory that pours from Jesus.*

That is certainly my experience to date. And it isn't just
with regard to physical or financial needs. While I was winc-
ing as the local anesthetic went in, I heard the voice of God
again, as a father would talk to a son, reassuring me that
beyond the cold and frightening walls of the medical imaging
department and beyond the realm of the visible, angels were
standing guard. That this fight is not mine; it's His. And while I
don't see it with my eyes, there is most definitely a war taking
place in the realm of the unseen. A war for my life and for the
well-being of my family. Each of us precious in the Father's
eyes. Each of us known intimately by Him.

I have called and He has answered.

Like He said He would.

When I walk into the hospital, scared of what the day
might bring, He knows.

When I sit down in the waiting room flicking through the
pictures of my wife and sons on my phone and tears fill my
eyes, He knows.

When the emotional strain of an entire day of medical
tests is piling up on me like a schoolyard rumble, He knows.

Nobody knows or understands me better.

Psalm 139:1–10 states:

You have searched me, LORD,
*   and you know me.*
You know when I sit and when I rise;
*   you perceive my thoughts from afar.*

You discern my going out and my lying down;
  you are familiar with all my ways.
Before a word is on my tongue
  you, LORD, know it completely.
You hem me in behind and before,
  and you lay your hand upon me.
Such knowledge is too wonderful for me,
  too lofty for me to attain.

Where can I go from your Spirit?
  Where can I flee from your presence?
If I go up to the heavens, you are there;
  if I make my bed in the depths, you are there.
If I rise on the wings of the dawn,
  if I settle on the far side of the sea,
even there your hand will guide me,
  your right hand will hold me fast.

So I move forward, one serious, life-saving step at a time, fully aware that my steps are shadowed by the fiercest of heaven's warriors, under the direct command of God Himself.

BRING THE RAIN

Today we up the ante.

Today we commence nuclear warfare.

The sun is rising, the house is silent, and I'm preparing myself mentally for the day ahead.

I am not feeling brave.

I am not feeling heroic.

I'm just a man doing what has to be done.

Any strength I have today comes from the knowledge that God is with me.

The surgeons have reviewed the strategy. The battle plans are confirmed. The nuclear weapons are ready and standing by.

You may see a solitary man walking the corridors of the hospital today, but if you look past the visible to the unseen, you'll see.

I've brought my own army.

Ten thousand of heaven's fiercest fighters. Itching for a fight.

Their commander?

God Himself.

We're comin' for ya, cancer.

Today.

Count on it.

SIRT – PART 3

The procedure went well.

Textbook.

It wasn't as uncomfortable (or as long) as the trial, though it was still weird feeling the catheter creeping through my body.

Having met everyone the week before made things so much easier when it came time for the real thing. It was like meeting friends. Lots of hellos and a few jokes from Dave again.

The hardest part was the thirty-six hours afterward. The doctor warned me I'd be in for "a rough night," but nothing prepared me for the level of pain that came during that time.

Unfortunately I had only been given codeine to assist with pain management. With this level of pain, the codeine was like candy and did absolutely nothing.

Note to self: next time, ask for narcotic-based painkillers.

I was radioactive for a week afterward and was not allowed to sleep in the same bed as Rachel or get too close to the boys. Thankfully, our friends Tony and Brenda provided me with a spare room in their house, which is just across the road from our home.

Presently, I am still recovering and will be for the next few weeks.

Very short attention span (hence the shorthand form of this update) and absolute exhaustion by about midday each day.

I sleep. Then I sleep some more. The next day I do it all over again.

Now we wait—three months—for results.

Here's a picture in case anyone is curious.

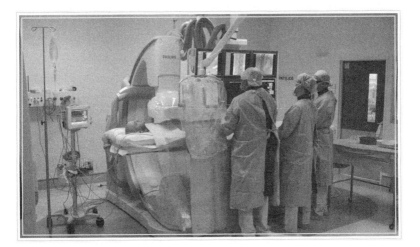

WONDERFUL INCONVENIENCE

Four years ago today I wrote the following.

4:00 p.m.: Phone rings.

Kristian: Hello?

Rachel: Hi, it's me. I think I'm in labor.

Kristian: What, now?!

Rachel: Yes, now.

Kristian: But it can't be now. It's two weeks early! We have to move house on the weekend, and we're still not packed, and ... this is really inconvenient. It's not supposed to be happening now!

Rachel: I know! But it's happening!

Kristian: OK ... I'll meet you at home in thirty minutes.

This photo was taken a few days after Cody was born.

6:00 p.m.: Arrive at the hospital with bags in tow, still thinking it may be a false alarm.

6:30 p.m.: Nope—it's the real deal. Already five centimeters dilated.

7:15 p.m.: Water breaks; contractions big-time.

9:00 p.m.: Midwife gives the all clear to start pushing.

10:10 p.m.: Little head pops out. (*Pops* is hardly the right word. It was well and truly pushed, hard.)

10:24 p.m.: Cody Israel Anderson takes his first breath.

Tonight I thanked God that I am not a woman. I have always respected women, but tonight *respect* has been redefined. My wife is amazing, and I am so unbelievably in awe of what she has just accomplished. So while she is sleeping, I am bouncing off the walls.

It's been a good week. I saw U2 three times in Sydney with the best seats in the house; the eclipse; I bought a new guitar; and now—now I have a son.

It doesn't get any better than this.

So welcome to the world, my wonderful little inconvenience.

Your daddy loves you very much.

This is Cody today.

Every day I thank God for this boy. How can I not fight when I have this to live for?

FROM RACHEL

I'm not a terribly inquisitive person, so I had no idea about the birthday video, none at all. Cody had said something at one point that made me think twice — something about Daddy taking him to the place with the lights. I knew there was a lighting shop next to the shop where Kristian bought my exercise bike, so I thought maybe they'd just gone to look at the lights.

A few weeks before, Kristian had asked what I knew of John Key, the New Zealand Prime Minister, and I said, "Oh, I don't know.

He got elected after I left the country. I think he's a nice guy ..." At that point Kristian had emailed John Key's PA at his local electoral office to ask if he would appear in the video, and he was waiting to hear back. He was just curious whether I thought he might be the sort of guy who would be nice enough to do something like that. But again, I had no idea that there was anything more at stake. It was just a question he was asking.

Before my birthday, there were a few times when he told me he needed to go Frame, Set & Match, the postproduction company where he used to work. That wasn't so extraordinary. There have been occasions when he's had to take work to them to get effects done. It did not cross my mind that it had anything to do with my birthday, but that's when he was getting the special effects done for my video—the card with the thunder and lightning, the shots where he was holding the card and I was walking down the aisle.

Kristian had organized this massive surprise party for me on the day of my birthday.He had lined up a caterer and a massive jumping castle for the boys, and I had no idea about that either. He had stayed home from church that morning, saying he wasn't feeling well when actually he was getting all the final details ready for the party. But the night before, he did show the video to me because he couldn't wait any longer. Originally he had planned to show it to me for the first time in front of everybody at the party, but then he decided he wanted me to see it on my own first.

It's pretty special. After that, Kristian would get recognized when we went out. Not long after he'd had his bowel surgery and got the colostomy bag, we were invited to a premiere for one of Russell Crowe's movies. We were standing in the line and someone came up to ask Kristian a question because they had recognized him. When we were in Disneyland, the video had been shown on *Oprah* just the week before, and within a half hour of being there, we were recognized by three different groups of people. It was more Kristian than me, because his face was the one that was on screen the most.

You could pretty much track where it had been aired all around the world, because Kristian would get a whole lot of comments on his blog site from Russia, and then a bunch from Poland, then England, and so on as it made its way around the world. It was quite a phenomenal thing.

Calling All Angels

BETTER DAYS

December 24, 2010

Better days indeed.

December 2010 has been full of them, and I am incredibly grateful.

On December 9, I had my first post-SIRT blood test. The test showed that not only was my liver functioning perfectly after the radioactive blast, but it also showed that after only four weeks, my cancer markers had decreased significantly — by 65 percent, in fact. On top of that, it was decided that I should have a three-month break from chemotherapy while the radiation continues to do its thing. I nearly cried at the sound of both of these bits of information, particularly the chemo rest. I have endured thirteen months of nonstop chemo, and I was finding it very difficult emotionally. To think that I might have a Christmas where I wasn't flat on my back, staring at the ceiling, and drifting in and out of consciousness, was just the best news I'd had in a long time. I get to be semi-normal this Christmas, and so far it feels pretty good.

On December 13, Rachel and I went to see U2 in Sydney. We had been given access to (RED) Zone tickets — part of the proceeds go to the AIDS charity (RED)—by a friend of mine, and when it came time to pay for them, I was told not to worry. These were not inexpensive tickets, not by a long shot, and yet they were given with a smile and a hug.

At the U2 concert

On December 14, we had the privilege of attending *The Oprah Winfrey Show* at the Sydney Opera House, which was pretty cool, and a few days later, Rachel's parents arrived from New Zealand for a visit, and we were able to get away up the coast to Port Stephens for some time in the sun.

Right now Rachel is wrapping the last of the kids' Christmas presents. They're in bed sleeping soundly after a big day, and I'm sure I'll be following soon. The radiation still makes me very tired for most of the day. They weren't kidding when they said I'd be tired like never before. I've certainly never experienced anything quite like it. But it's OK; it means the radiation is working.

So much amazing stuff has happened to us this month (some I can't talk about yet; you'll have to wait and see) that most of the time I'm having to stop and check if it is actually happening.

I see such momentum building. A kinetic energy that is nearly unstoppable because it has the force of heaven behind it. I don't understand the way things are unfolding but I can clearly see the hand of God in all of it, and even though I know it to be true, sometimes I still can't quite believe it.

I don't know how to pray a holy prayer or how to conduct myself before Almighty God. I swear sometimes. If you cut me off in traffic, I'll probably flip you the bird. And if you threaten my wife or kids, I'll probably give you a black eye. I'm a walking contradiction.

But despite all of my character flaws (and yes, there are many), God has been answering my cry for help, almost daily. Long before I knew what kind of help I needed, He had already set the wheels in motion. Like a trail of dominoes carefully laid out, things are falling into place, one after the other, with such precision and timing that at times I have to pinch myself.

Every day I see God keeping His promises to me. Not in a way I would ever have expected, but still so far and above what I could even imagine. All of this is just the start. You're going to see something miraculous take place here; I can feel it. In fact, I'd bet my life on it. You're going to witness the

God of heaven reach into my life and do something that's never been seen before. Not because I'm special. I've already told you I'm not. But because of His compassion and mercy, because of His great love for me.

You're going to see it, and you're going to know He did it.

BITTER/SWEET

December was pretty good, so I should have expected January to bite back—hard.

It did.

With Kristian's parents, Sandy and Andy, and his sister, Bethany, six weeks before Kristian died

We went to Perth in Western Australia to spend a couple of weeks with my parents for Christmas and New Year. Not long after arriving, I began to feel a little off-color. I would break out in sweat or start shivering; I wasn't keeping much food down and mostly didn't feel like eating anyway; and to top it all off, the heat in Perth was seriously oppressive. There were a string of one-hundred-degree-Fahrenheit days shortly after our arrival, which made it pretty much impossible to do anything comfortably.

After a little while, I was beginning to worry I had pneumonia. I had all the symptoms, and it is a known side effect of the SIRT, so I took myself to the doctor to get it checked out. Thankfully, chest X-rays showed it was not pneumonia. So what was it?

Two days later I got my first clue: blood in the toilet. It was the bowel tumor.

Fast-forward a few days, and we're back home in Sydney. I'm feeling worse than before, so I head up to the oncology ward to see my nurses. CT scans are ordered and confirm what everyone thought: the tumor had grown and was now blocking the bowel. And by *blocking*, I mean it was packed. I'm admitted immediately and the surgeon is called. Before the day is out, I am scheduled for emergency bowel surgery the next morning.

It's serious. Life-threatening, in fact.

The morning of the surgery, I am prepped as best as I possibly can be. This "preparation" comes in the form of a barium enema. Just lovely. Then it's back into bed to wait for Rachel to arrive before heading down to the operating room. I wasn't going anywhere without her.

Rachel arrives, and we start to get a bit teary. I'm afraid, and so is she. We cannot get a clear answer on what to expect, because the doctors themselves don't know. They're working with the information provided by the scans and won't know exactly what they're dealing with until they cut me open, right down the middle.

We get to the operating room, and it's me, the surgeon, and the anesthetist. I know the surgeon. He took my appendix out years ago and also performed the colonoscopy that found the tumor in the first place. I ask him for the truth, and he gives it to me, straight-out.

This is an emergency procedure with an unprepared bowel (read: full to the limit). It's going to be messy. There's an 80 percent chance I'm going to lose my entire large colon. In fact, it's almost guaranteed. The tumor is very close to some important arteries, so it's quite unlikely they will attempt to remove it. It's too risky. And there's a 5 percent chance I *won't* need a colostomy bag for the rest of my life. That's just how it is. He's sorry, but he doesn't really have a choice.

Now it's just me in the corridor.

God?

Help.

Please, God, no colostomy bag, no taking of my large colon. Please. Please. Please.

Please do something.

Rachel comes in; we're both crying. I tell her how much I love her and to make sure the boys know how much their daddy loved them, just in case I don't wake up. The nurse leads her away in tears, and I'm wheeled inside.

Heavy eyes.

Out.

The next thing I remember is hearing Rachel's voice and the beeping of the heart-rate monitor. I can't open my eyes, can't move my body, but I can feel her hand holding mine. I try to squeeze it to let her know I'm here. It works. She feels it.

I made it.

As the days progress, I am allowed nothing by mouth. (All total, seven days, so I lost a lot of weight.) It's not until about day two or three post-op that Rachel tells me what has happened.

The nurse rang her as soon as the surgery was over. She said they were totally surprised when they opened me up. Things were not entirely as they appeared on the scan. They inspected the bowel for signs of more cancer and found none, so they proceeded to remove the tumor from my bowel as it was—and they got the whole thing.

My bowel is now cancer free.

There are a string of events leading up to this operation that, in isolation, just appear to be random events. When you put them together and realize what each event means in relation to the other, it's very, very clear:

I called. God answered.

After going through another ten days' recovery in the hospital, I am home and on the mend.

Bitter?

It will be a slow and painful recovery, and I will have a bag for two months. I have what's known as a stoma: my bowel exit now appears next to my belly button. It's like looking at a cheap horror movie with my insides actually outside. The bag needs changing daily, and it's incredibly confronting for me. I've also never experienced physical pain like this before. I'm getting better but am on a reasonable pain-management regimen for the next few weeks: morphine, etc. I can't pick anything up, and the stomach wound is very, very tender. This means contact with Cody and Jakob must be limited to protect myself. Very, very hard to deal with.

Sweet?

The stoma is totally reversible and only temporary. My bowel will be put back together and will function naturally again. What was expected to be a worst-case situation has turned around entirely overnight to be the best possible outcome.

And the sweetest of all is that my bowel cancer is now gone.

I'm going to let you draw your own conclusions as to what has happened here, but in my mind's eye, I see my God standing at the foot of my bed. He nods silently, with a surety that only my Creator can have. And I am reminded of this:

For I am the LORD, your God,
who takes hold of your right hand
and says to you, Do not fear;
I will help you.

ISAIAH 41:13

HUMBLED

We've had to keep quiet about all of this (as much as possible, anyway) until the show went to air.

Our lives have been profoundly impacted by the compassion and generosity of Oprah Winfrey and her Harpo team along with Microsoft and Xbox Australia. They have made it possible for me to focus my energy on getting well and for Rachel to take time off work and focus on our family by giving us an incredibly generous gift of money.

Let me just say, every person we have had the pleasure of meeting and dealing with on our way to the Opera House and beyond has shown us how beautiful humanity can be when it sets its heart on helping others.

I am encouraged and inspired to be a better man and to mimic this kind of generosity in my own life. If you only knew the path we have walked to this point. One day I'll explain it all.

To everyone who kept us in the dark (!) and gave us the surprise of our lives (massive understatement), we are so truly blessed to know you and look forward to seeing you again.

Dinner is on us!

ONCOLOGY (AND OTHER BLACK ARTS)

Today has been a pretty bad day.

I went up to the hospital to see my oncologist for the first time since my bowel surgery and, to be honest, was expecting good news. I mean, the bowel cancer was now gone and the liver cancer had been served an eviction notice by the SIR procedure, so in theory it should have been smiles.

It wasn't.

Surprise, disappointment, shock—not what we expected at all.

My CEA markers have jumped from 600-ish to 2,890. That's almost a 500 percent increase. My CA 19-9 has also jumped from 72 back to 112. Apart from the overwhelming feeling of crushing defeat I was feeling, I was also wondering how on earth it happened. I'm asking everyone I know who might know *something*, but nobody can give me an answer. It could be this or this or that; we don't know. But whatever it is, it's definitely a shock to everyone involved.

My biggest concern is: what if it has spread to another part of my body?

Forward from here? I start a new treatment regimen in two weeks on a drug called Erbitux (Cetuximab). It's supposed to be an amazing drug. Another in the biologic realm rather than chemical. Its main side effect is an acne-like rash in all the places one would normally get acne, so I'm probably going to regress twenty years and start looking like some pizza-faced teenager over the coming weeks and months. Just wonderful.

Over the past six weeks I feel like I have been dropped

into a fight circle, and no matter which way I turn, I am being pummeled from all sides. I turn one direction—whack. Turn the other direction—whack. I just don't seem to be able to get a break from the constant hammering of scalpels, needles, stitches, staples, drugs—the list goes on, seemingly forever.

And of course the fact that nobody can shed any light on the reasons my markers have jumped so severely means that once again our lives go into an indefinite holding pattern.

I swear, if cancer were a person right now, I would snap its neck. I feel so robbed, so cheated. I am trying so hard here. I am doing *everything* I am told to do, regardless of what it does to my body and my mind. They say; I do. There's no question. And if, for the tiniest of milliseconds, my mind forgets, then my heart quickly steps up and fills the gap.

Why?

Rachel.

Cody.

Jakob.

Son of David ... Jesus ... have mercy. I don't know how much more I can take.

QUACK, QUACK

I should call this *Dress Code Part 2*, but it goes beyond that for me right now.

If it walks like a duck and talks like a duck, then it is a duck. Or in my case, if it walks like a fake and talks like a fake, then it is a fake.

I don't like to use my blog for this kind of thing, but as it is becoming more frequent, I feel I need to draw a line in the sand and make my position very clear.

If you are not a doctor or qualified medical personnel, if you do not have the letters MD or PhD at the end of your name, and if you do not legally practice medicine day in, day out—keep your distance. I am so tired of hearing people tell me that my doctors are withholding information from me, that they are in cahoots with the big pharmacy companies, and that between them and the Australian government, they actually have a cure for cancer but are keeping it hidden in order to make billions of dollars from the suffering of countless cancer patients.

Last night was the final straw. I was told I would be "an idiot" to continue chemotherapy and that it was "a miracle the chemo had not killed me yet." All this from someone who has no qualifications and who continually ducked my requests to provide clarification as to what it is they were offering and what their qualifications were. Some of the "information" offered was so ludicrous it does not bear repeating. Suffice to say, I had it shot down by two doctor friends of mine within seconds of the phone call. But of course, I can't trust them— they're being paid off by the big pharmacies.

Give me a break.

I'm not going to try and counter such idiocy with a logical and rational argument. I don't have the time or the energy, but if you're one of the fruity few who actually believe this kind of rubbish and go around trying to convert others to your cause, know this: you are causing great harm by repeating it to those who are fighting cancer. I would go so far as to say your behavior is predatory, because the people you target are often in very vulnerable and fragile positions, both mentally and physically.

Well, enough. You have been warned. Come at me again with this crap, and you will see a very different Kristian Anderson. The one who will do what it takes to defend himself and his family. The one who will forget politeness and courtesy, the one who will bust you open like a melon on a rock and expose you for the fraud you are.

This is *my* life you're trying to gamble with here, and I won't have any part in your quackery.

Do I make myself clear?

GARDENING

I have a lot of different voices in my ear most days. There's the medical opinions, the "fake medical conspiracy" opinions, the voices of good friends ringing to see how I am, the voice of fear that comes in whenever things don't look so good to the human eye. And then there's my own voice—my thoughts. Many times my own thoughts are like ten thousand crossed telephone wires, and it's a real struggle to still them.

In times like these, I have to listen carefully for the one voice that will never force itself into my world. The voice that will not huff and puff and stomp away if it goes unheeded. The voice that will speak to me, oh so softly, until I come around. The still, small voice of the Spirit of God.

I have been walking a rough path for the last eighteen months or so now. Anyone who has endured cancer treatment will understand immediately the agony of this path, not only in your own body and life, but also in the lives of those who love you. But in the middle of all of that, I have learned to recognize the quiet voice of God. To date, it has not let me down or steered me in the wrong direction. It brings peace and comfort and allows me a chance to breathe, when the reality of my world would seek to crush the very air from my lungs.

And so I'm making sure this is the one voice that doesn't get ignored. I'm weeding out the voices, no matter how well intentioned, that would bring harm, and allowing only those that bring hope and peace. I know there are still those who would call me naive, ignorant, or even "idiotic," as one lovely soul put it. But you know what? I don't care.

My house, my rules. It's my garden, and I decide what grows in it.

And in the center of that garden, I choose to plant myself right by the unfailing word of God.

Jeremiah 17:7–8 states:

> ... *blessed is the one who trusts in the* LORD,
>   *whose confidence is in him.*
> *They will be like a tree planted by the water*
>   *that sends out its roots by the stream.*
> *It does not fear when heat comes;*
>   *its leaves are always green.*
> *It has no worries in a year of drought*
>   *and never fails to bear fruit.*

I have no idea what the future holds, but I know that if I am anchored with deep roots, whatever comes can huff and puff, yet when it's all said and done, I will still be standing strong. My hope lies not in doctors or medicine, though I am very grateful for the help they bring. My hope, my confidence, is in the God of heaven.

He does not and cannot lie.

Watch and see.

I WANT A NEW DRUG

I had new CT scans done this week and got a chance to sit down with my oncologist to review them.

I was due for these scans anyway, as it has been three months since the SIR-Spheres procedure and the results would show how effective (or not) it had been. With the surprise blood results from a few weeks back, they were also needed for my peace of mind.

And ... the scans show no signs that the cancer has spread.

Good news.

They also show that the remaining tumors in my liver have calcified. My oncologist explained that this generally means the tumors are inactive. Where there had been "room" inside them before due to the fact they were living organisms, they have since died off. The body then fills the space with calcium deposits to help protect and heal the affected area. At least that's how I understand it. If anyone (qualified) would like to comment and explain it further, I'd be happy to hear it. But you must be a doctor or nurse, OK? On top of that, the tests that look at liver function are showing a significant decrease in all areas—another good sign.

I'm now on the drug named Erbitux and have received two infusions so far. I'm responding, or so we think, because

I have broken out in some terribly painful acne all over my head and torso. As painful as it is, it's usually a sign that the drug is doing its thing. I'm grateful it appears to be working, but the acne and rash are very itchy and cause my scalp to burn. I am constantly going to the bathroom to stick my head under a cold shower to try and achieve some kind of relief. It's impossible to lay my head on my pillow, so I am now waiting until I can't stay awake any longer to crash from exhaustion in order to get some sleep at night. I have antibiotics and cream, so hopefully they will assist in making things more bearable.

Between the itching and burning scalp, the stoma, and the neuropathy (still constant pins and needles, especially in feet; curse you, Oxaliplatin), I am struggling to remember what it feels like to have a "normal" body. When Huey Lewis sang "I Want a New Drug" and specified medication that would not make him talk too much or make his face break out, he wasn't far off the mark. But it's temporary, and the end results, i.e., not dying, are worth it if it means I am here for decades to come.

My CEA markers are still very high (up to 4,000) but my CA 19-9 has not moved since we checked it a few weeks back. It's holding up at 112. My oncologist is confident that once the Erbitux begins to work through the body, these numbers should begin to come down. It would be strange indeed if they do not, given there is no bowel cancer anymore and the liver is looking the best it has in a very long time.

One day, all of this will be a distant memory, recognizable but unfamiliar.

This week, I picked up one of my guitars, my black Duesenberg 49er, for the first time in a very long time. I went through a stage where I did not really care if I ever played or produced music again. I was saddened by my loss of passion for music, but at the same time, I felt powerless to stop it from fading. But after seeing Train up close and being able to see the joy on Jimmy Stafford's face as he played, I was reminded of what it felt like to lean back into the music and get lost in the moment. I know the feeling well; it's just been a while. My hands held up OK, so this week I'm going to start working on a new pedal board and try to get back into scales to jog my finger memory.

It feels nice to play again. Hopefully the neighbors won't mind.

By the way, a big welcome to Oprah's 302 "ultimate viewers"—the fans who came along to Australia with Oprah in December. I really appreciate you taking the time to stop by.

DORSA

I've been sitting on this for a few weeks now as I have found it moves me quite a lot to think about it, even weeks later.

By the end of the first week and mid-second week of Erbitux infusions, I was in considerable discomfort, thanks to the rash and acne on my head. It was nearly unbearable. I tried to escape it, but it followed me everywhere. Rachel suggested I go to the pharmacy for some antihistamine tablets, so I jumped in the car and headed off right away. The weather has been nice and cool here in Sydney the past few weeks, and I found myself driving with the window down, the cool breeze passing over my burning head and relieving some of my discomfort.

I arrived at the pharmacy, and as I was standing in line, a young woman approached me and, with an accent, proceeded to ask very timidly if I was "from *Oprah*." I told her that I was, and she smiled an enormous smile. She told me she had multiple sclerosis and that for a long time, she had been battling serious depression. She told me that after seeing our story on *The Oprah Winfrey Show*, she was so deeply moved and encouraged and her depression left her. She then thanked me for my courage and for helping her; she told me that without me, she would still be suffering depression.

And I'm just standing there, conscious of the other customers watching us out of the corner of my eye, desperately trying not to cry, so humbled. Standing there being told by a complete stranger that my own fight is helping them with theirs.

She reached out and shook my hand. We exchanged pleasantries, and then she went back into the doctor's office next door to wait with her sister.

On my way home, I had to pull the car over to the side of the road as I was overcome with emotion, the scene playing out in my mind again and again. I began to weep. There was such an overpowering feeling that I had been a part of a very sacred transaction. All of this—the cancer, the fight, the pain, the discomfort, the not knowing, all of it—it's not for me, not for my benefit.

It's for others.

I truly had my eyes opened to a very small but powerful reality that night. I don't know how to explain it, but I feel incredibly privileged to have been able to glimpse just a piece of it. Seeing how God can use something as awful as my cancer to release others is just overwhelming.

In so many ways, cancer is the most awful experience, but at times like this, it feels like such a gift.

Please pray for this young lady. Her name is Dorsa. She's from Persia and can't be more than twenty-five years old.

She's far too young to be facing a life battling MS.

MANY HANDS

Right now in Australia the federal government is dragging its heels in relation to releasing the drug Erbitux onto the PBS. The Pharmaceutical Benefits Advisory Committee and the board of Medicare have both signed off and given it the thumbs-up, and the government has promised to release it to those who need it. But they haven't done it by the date they said they would, and we're not getting any answers as to when they intend to honor their promise.

Erbitux is working wonders in my body. I kid you not.

I have been on the drug for eight weeks now (I had my eighth infusion yesterday) and today received my round seven results. In just seven weeks, my CEA markers have dropped from 4,100 to 234. My CA 19-9 markers have dropped from 113 to 13.9. Remember that in the CA 19-9 arena, a "normal" person has a marker count of 37 and below. Each week, my markers decrease by 25 to 50 percent. At a time when my markers were inexplicably climbing, Erbitux has sent them packing. Keep in mind the success of the bowel operation and the SIR-Spheres treatment, but still, it's producing incredible results. Erbitux needs to be, *must* be, available as a frontline treatment option.

There are approximately two thousand Australians who need Erbitux. My weekly treatment costs $2,000 to supply. All up, we need $30 million dollars a year to potentially bring this kind of result to many, many Australians at no cost to themselves.

The government has promised it, but I need all of you to help remind them of their pledge to the cancer patients of Australia.

When I first started this journey, my voice was small, quiet, and helpless. Today my voice echoes loudly around the world, thanks to the prayers and support of everyone who visits the blog, countless prayer groups and churches around the world, the local media here in Australia, news outlets around the globe, and, of course, Oprah.

We can make a difference. One person plus one person plus one person ... all of us little people. I'm convinced of it.

The benefits I am receiving from this drug should be available to everyone who needs it. It's not a miracle cure, but it is really smart science—and it works.

It works.

CLAY AND WATER

I'm tired, again. Really tired.

Physically—very slow. Mentally—dull and listless.

I just had my twenty-ninth chemo infusion, and while the Erbitux is easy to cope with compared to my original Avastin and Oxaliplatin regimen, it's still a hard slog. The Oxaliplatin has left me with considerable nerve damage in my feet and toes. A drop in temperature of even only a few degrees can be enough to make standing or walking unbearable, and that's assuming it wasn't a cold day to start with. But I love a cold day, because the cooler air is soothing on my head and torso. The rash from the Erbitux is subdued by cooler temperatures, and the burning somehow becomes bearable.

There's no such thing as in-between when it comes to cancer. It's cards down and guns drawn; all in or you're dead.

Rock, meet hard place.

And in all of this, I am still trying to understand the whys and the why nots. So many things I just don't understand.

Before cancer, I was pretty ambitious, to a fault. I was driven, but I was driving myself toward things that held no eternal value, no lasting satisfaction. I tolerated certain situations that took me away from my family and allowed my boundaries to be compromised. I tolerated certain people in the foolish belief that they might open doors for my future, all the while knowing they were the kind of people I didn't want to be like. All in the name of success. But cancer has stripped away the things inside me that sought to benefit only my immediate family and myself. These things I thought I could not do without are now cast aside on the road through the valley.

I see a lot of discarded things on this road. Things thrown away by people who have walked the road before me and have come to the same revelatory realization, our understanding of eternal things accelerated by our own imminent demise. The deepest cry for mercy bringing with it the deepest understanding.

To the human eye we become "victims," "sufferers."

Weak.

Sick.

Sad.

Pitied.

We become nothing.

Our brokenness is repulsive to those who have apparently got it all together. And yet, the more broken we become, the more cracks that appear, the more light that gets in.

I am nothing. I have always said this. This journey is not about me. It's not to show you how strong I am, for my strength comes from God. It's not to show you how great my faith is, for my faith is a gift from God. And it's not to show you how courageous I am, for my courage comes from God, exactly at the time I need it. Anything you see in me that is good is not of my doing; it's from heaven. I'm not the well-respected religious leader. I'm not the upstanding citizen. I'm not the guy who's got it all together. I'm the tax collector in Luke 18:9–14 (MSG):

> *"Two men went up to the Temple to pray, one a Pharisee, the other a tax man. The Pharisee posed and prayed like this: 'Oh, God, I thank you that I am not like other people—robbers, crooks, adulterers, or, heaven forbid, like this tax man. I fast twice a week and tithe on all my income.'"*
>
> *"Meanwhile the tax man, slumped in the shadows, his face in his hands, not daring to look up, said, 'God, give mercy. Forgive me, a sinner.'"*

Jesus commented, "This tax man, not the other, went home made right with God. If you walk around with your nose in the air, you're going to end up flat on your face, but if you're content to be simply yourself, you will become more than yourself."

You will become more than yourself...

Maybe I'm Superman. Or maybe I'm just on the receiving end of a merciful God's gift.

I am constantly reminded of how broken I really am. My body doesn't work the way it's supposed to. It's doing things it shouldn't and is being subjected to ongoing brutality as we attempt to correct its behavior. My mortality has never been more obvious, and I am reminded daily that if God does not intervene in my situation, I'm a dead man. And that's just the physical brokenness. I could write page after page about my own frail humanity. But it's what Christ offers me, to fix it once and for all, that turns the liability into an asset. To replace my weakness with His strength. To offer Himself in my place.

This journey from who I was to who I was born to be, this *becoming*, is not a path I would have willingly chosen for myself or for those who love me. Believe me, it's painful. My body aches almost as much as my heart, and whether or not it has been chosen for me is open to much debate. But it doesn't matter. I'm being shaped, regardless. Thrown down onto the Potter's wheel as He digs His hands in and squeezes out the imperfections, placed into the fire to seal the skilled handiwork. All the while having no idea what I'm supposed to be, what I'm becoming. Trusting in the One leading me; trusting Him for my very life.

Not long after we were married, with my brothers and sisters

CALLING ALL ANGELS

We had a family holiday in New Zealand these past few weeks. Rachel and the boys headed over on a Sunday, and I joined them the following Wednesday after another chemotherapy session. The boys love going to NZ, as they get to see their two younger cousins as well as their nanna and poppa and uncles and aunties. It's also an incredibly valuable time for Rachel to recharge and just be in a familiar place with people who know her best.

We went down to a little beachside town called Onemana (pronounced Oh-Knee-Mah-Nah), which is near the town of Whangamata (pronounced Fung-Ah-Ma-Tah), for a weekend away with Rachel's brothers and her sister and their spouses and kids. We stayed in a house owned by some relatives of Rachel's, and it was pretty crowded. Our little family stayed in the converted garage, which is separated from the main house by a twenty-foot walkway, while everyone else stayed in the main house.

After dinner one night, it comes bedtime for Cody and Jakob. They say good night to everyone, and we take them to our room, where they watch a movie on the portable TV/DVD combo we bought for the times when we travel (soon to be replaced with an iPad). It doesn't take long until both boys crash out and are sleeping peacefully, so we put them into bed, said our prayers, and lay with them for a bit while they slept. After a while, we headed back inside to join the rest of the gang—me first, then Rachel. As usual, one of us goes back in periodically to check on them to make sure everything is OK. It was my turn this time, so off I went, thinking everything would be fine.

It wasn't.

After trying to get back to the main house and deciding it was too dark and scary to walk the twenty feet between the dwellings, the two boys had locked themselves in the en suite bathroom and were crying their little hearts out. When I got inside, I found them standing, with Cody up front and Jakob clinging to Cody's leg, terrified and sobbing.

"Daddy, we couldn't find you! We were lonely," Cody sobbed.

"Yeah," Jakob agreed through teary eyes.

I knelt down in front of them and they ran into my arms, their little bodies heaving. I wrapped my arms around them and told them everything was all right now. Daddy was here.

Cody again looked into my eyes and said: "We called out for you, but you didn't come. We were all alone."

And then it hit me . . . and I started softly crying with them. I crumpled into them as much as they had crumpled into me. Rach came in right about then, and we all hugged and explained to Mummy what had happened. I was still fighting tears as we climbed back into bed and rubbed their backs and played with their hair to settle them back down. We stayed with them until they fell asleep.

As the days since that moment have passed, I have had something gnawing at my insides, like something just isn't right. I've been playing the scene over and over in my head, and the memory of their little faces, sad and afraid, upsets me deeply. And the other day it hit me.

Cody is incredibly intelligent and has a large vocabulary. He knows words and is very capable of expressing himself clearly in most situations. What has absolutely shaken me are the words he used to tell me what was wrong: *"We were lonely." "We couldn't find you." "We were all alone."*

And I realized that this is what they will say if I die.

And the worst part is, I won't be able to put my arms around them and tell them that Daddy is here; it's going to be all right. And we won't have big family hugs where the boys are comforted and reassured that Mummy and Daddy love them very much and are here to protect them, and that will be the way it is for them for the rest of their lives. While I will pass instantly into eternity—where there is no sadness or pain or sorrow or fear—Cody, Jakob, and Rachel will live out their days on earth—full and productive days, but with a sadness buried deep inside them. Beautiful little boys, growing up into fine young men, without their father. Rachel forging on, without her husband and friend, and it kills me inside to think of it.

And as I sat down in the oncology ward to receive my thirtieth infusion yesterday, I again sat down with one purpose:

To fight.

Fighting for my life. Fighting for my wife and sons.

As I unbuttoned my shirt, as the needle went into my port, as the saline went in and the blood came out, as the Erbitux made its way into my body to do battle with my cancer, as the clock on the wall reminded me how long it all takes, every week—the fight.

Every second of burning, itching, and mutated skin—the fight. Every damaged nerve ending—the fight. Every hour hunched over the toilet bowl, puking my guts out—the fight. Every scar, every incision—the fight. Every time I see Death standing in my bedroom doorway at night—the fight.

In "War of My Life," John Mayer calls out the angels and the ghosts; he's in the war of his life, he says, with no choice but to fight "'til it's done."

And so I do. Until the cancer is dead—or I am.

And there will be casualties along the way.

Because that's how it is in a war.

THE GOOD, THE BAD, AND THE UGLY

Yesterday was chemo round thirty-four. It always hits me later in the evening, around 7:00 p.m. Heavy-duty tiredness, to the point where keeping my eyes open is a major effort. I imagine my head like the top of a tree in a storm, moving back and forth erratically, while my body remains motionless. Just the top being pushed around at will. But there's minimal nausea, which is nice.

The good:

So far things are going along as they should. I'm still receiving treatment—Erbitux weekly. I still have cancer, but I'm not dying. It's under control, as much as the medical fraternity and modern pharmaceuticals can control it anyway. The Dexamethasone they give me during the infusion suppresses the majority of the nausea and makes my skin manageable for the first day or so afterward. Through the process of elimination, I've determined it's the Dex that settles it down. I mentioned this to my oncologist, and he was happy to prescribe a daily dose in tablet form.

My liver enzyme markers are all down, some back within normal tolerances, which is very good. Considering my liver is the only place the cancer still has a hold, this is a good sign. My liver is functioning perfectly. My CA 19-9 markers are holding steady at 11.1, well within normal, and my CEA markers are bouncing around week to week between 143 and the latest round of 174, which is still good compared to when they were over 4,000. It represents a decrease of about 96 percent since we started on the Erbitux. Unfortunately, instead of decreases of hundreds of points per round, we're now only seeing decreases in the five- to ten-point range. Not bad in and of itself; the numbers are still trending in the right direction, but I have a feeling the last 4 percent is going to be a very hard-fought battle. Assuming the math stays the same and it drops by five points each time, we're still looking at another thirty or so rounds before I'm safe. Fifteen if it goes down in multiples of ten. Sigh.

The bad:

I'm still having treatment weekly. It's really starting to get me down. There just doesn't seem to be any end in sight. We're locked firmly into that dreaded holding pattern with very little room to move. All I can do is keep showing up for treatment, keep looking for new ways to manage the pain and irritation on my skin—and just keep knocking on heaven's door. I've been feeling particularly low this week and last, as I have managed to pick up a case of shingles. Apparently once you have chicken pox, a form of the virus stays in your body for life, hiding itself in the nerve endings in your spine. It usually only manifests itself if the body is run down or the immune system is less than stellar. I qualify on both counts. Shingles, as anyone who has had them will attest, is incredibly painful.

My oncologist has offered me daily doses of Dex for my skin. The Dex really brings out the worst in me, more so after eighteen months' worth. Given that Mr. Hyde spends far too much time in our house as it is already, I have refused the offer. I just can't do it to Rach and the boys. As much as I desperately want relief from the burning and the itching and the pain, I can't do it.

I don't imagine for one second that any of this is anywhere near tolerable for Rachel. I'm not the man she married, that's for sure. Just how bad it is for her I don't quite know yet.

Cody is starting to become aware in his own way that something isn't quite right, and the other night as I was putting Jakob to bed, he grabbed my face with both hands, pulled me in close so we were nose to nose, looked me in the eye, and said, "Yooouu … Go. See. Da doctor." Then he kissed me and rolled over.

So ... no Dex tablets.

The ugly:

Me.

I hate having to look into the mirror. I see red, blotchy skin and swollen eyes. I see a torso covered in spots, a stomach with a stoma and colostomy bag, spotty arms and legs and feet with no feeling and a permanent sensation of pins and needles. I have never really been overly concerned with how I look. I think I gave up on that once I realized I was going bald, around the age of twenty or so. Nothing I could do about it, so why fight it? At the time I was dating a girl who didn't seem to mind (or at least she never told me if she did), and Rachel has never known me with hair. I've always done the Peter Garrett in the time she's known me. In fact, I think she actually prefers me bald than with hair.

But my self-image is under massive pressure. I really can't stand to look at myself. I get looks walking down the street, and I never know if it's because maybe someone has recognized me from *Oprah* or various TV and print media stories, or whether they're looking at me in horror, like some kind of mutant. I fully expect the mutant response because that's how I view myself. But like I said, this is war, and there are casualties along the way. I guess my ego needs a bullet or two.

Anyway, that's where I'm at right now. I get distracted easily, so my ability to hold any kind of decent conversation is limited. This includes conversations with God. I get quite frustrated that I can't sustain any kind of meaningful prayer with Him; it really bugs me. But it's times like these I just go back to the last thing He said to me:

I am the LORD your God
  who takes hold of your right hand
and says to you, Do not fear;
  I will help you.

ISAIAH 41:13

I know I'm still on His radar. So is Rachel. So is Cody. So is Jakob.

I firmly believe the time will come when I am safe from this disease. My healing has been sent; it's traveling, and at the appointed time, I will arrive in the same place at the same time as my healing.

In the meantime, it's back into the trenches.

FROM RACHEL

The whole *Oprah* experience was just mind-boggling, and I'm glad throughout the last two years we had moments like that. The producers told us we were going to be on the show for a segment about YouTube sensations, and we had no idea it was going to be anything more than that. Then we met Russell Crowe in the greenroom afterward, and we were invited to his Christmas party, and all these crazy things happened. I mean, who does that? Who are we to be mingling with such people? It felt so surreal for so long. We got to meet the band Train on the *Sunrise* show when they came to Australia, and they gave us tickets to their concert. I got to talk to them again afterward, and we have stayed in contact with them. It was a ridiculously good bubble in the middle of it all.

With Russell Crowe in the greenroom after *The Oprah Winfrey Show*

The side effects of Erbitux, this wonder drug that Kristian was campaigning to get put on the Pharmaceutical Benefit Scheme, were truly hideous. When he was on it, he felt quite strong physically, but he had pus-filled pimples covering his shoulders, up over his face, and all over the top of his head.

They looked just awful, and he was so uncomfortable. He felt like a freak. There were many times when it all felt too much, and he would say to me, "If it weren't for you and the boys, I don't think I could keep fighting." Even back then we had a few scares, and there were times when a part of me wanted to say, "Kristian, if you're ready to go, just go."

We knew it would be his decision in the end, that he would

reach a point and say, "God, I can't do this anymore," and his time would be up. I didn't want him hanging on just for us when he was so miserable. I was so glad he fought as long as he did, but you don't want to be the reason somebody is feeling so sick all the time. It was hard. It was so hard.

Dead Man Walking

THE STALKER

June 9, 2011

Death has been shadowing me the last few weeks.

I see him, not in my mind's eye, not in a vision, but with my eyes open, standing in my doorway at night. He just stares, silently, and doesn't move. He looks like you might imagine — a Dementor from the Harry Potter stories, a Ring Wraith from Lord of the Rings, or as the typical heavy-metal album or biker tattoo might depict him. Or a combination of all of them.

I'm sure you're hearing the sound of marbles rolling around on the floor, but I know what I see.

My markers are rising again.

My CA 19-9s are staying put around the 11 to 12 mark, but my CEAs have risen at each blood test for the past four weeks.

$158 \rightarrow 178 \rightarrow 184 \rightarrow 209 \ldots$ They're trending upward again. Of course there could be a whole bunch of reasons. Maybe the recent bout of shingles has something to do with it. They're still hanging around and still quite painful. Maybe my body just can't fight them both.

My body aches. Every day. It burns. It itches. It hurts.

The one thing that can bring all the burning and itching under control, the Dexamethasone, will likely destroy any sanity I have left if I take it in the doses needed to suppress the skin inflammation caused by the Erbitux. It will also likely destroy my family in the process by turning me into a permanent Mr. Hyde, changing me from David Banner into the not-so-incredible Hulk, so it's not an option.

And every night Death comes to my doorway and stares at me. I know he's not allowed any closer than the doorway to our room, but it still pisses me off that he's in my house at all.

I'm growing so weary of fighting.

Fighting my illness.

Fighting the side effects.

Fighting stupid, arrogant Christians who tell me I'm doing "jack-all for the kingdom of God."

Fighting the government to release Erbitux onto the PBS.

Fighting my own inner demons.

So tired.

I'm not gonna write
about the way things have been,
'cause lately they haven't been so great.
I keep falling down. I keep giving in.
I'm scared this is my fate.

If this is all that life would be,
if this is all there was for me,
I would not go on ...

I'm not gonna lie about feeling fine
and knowing everything's OK.

I've just got to believe that His hope inside
will lead me to a better place.

With every tear that I cry
I cling to the hope that will not die
He won't leave me here.

I will not lay down. This won't be my end.

MARGARET BECKER, "I WILL NOT LAY DOWN"

BE CAREFUL WHAT YOU WISH FOR ...

... you just might get it.

It's been a pretty overwhelming week.

I got a phone call on Tuesday morning, about 8:00 a.m., from a man I have had the pleasure of coming to know over the past few months. He's been so supportive of me and my attempts to get our government to list Erbitux on the PBS. He told me he didn't want to get my hopes up, but he'd heard a rumor that today might bring the good news we'd been waiting for.

Sure enough, at 9:00 a.m. he called me back. The federal government had committed $200 million to subsidize Erbitux and a number of other drugs for the thousands of Australians in desperate need of them.

Complete about-face.

As of September 1, 2011, Erbitux will cost $35.50 a week instead of $2,000 a week.

The cynics and the critics may say all they hear is wasted money, but I hear hope. I hear the collective sigh of relief from two thousand Australians who could not afford Erbitux, who could not afford to fight for their lives. People just like me, giving it all they've got and then some.

It was all over the news, how that guy who had cancer, who made that video that was on *Oprah*, who had been campaigning to get his drug on the PBS had … won. And there were photos and interviews and front pages and lots of smiles and some tears too.

But you need to know that while it may have been my face on the TV and in the newspapers, it wasn't just because of me that all this happened. There are people who would probably not think twice about seeking recognition for the role they played, and that's exactly why they deserve it.

That man I told you about earlier? Chris Reason, Channel 7 journalist. From the beginning, he took my voice and made it louder. I trust him. He listened.

The *Sunrise* program on 7; *The Today Show* on 9; *Kerri-Anne*, the morning show; *6.30 with George Negus*; Alan Jones at 2GB (the man whose tongue can start fires); Jason Morrison at 2UE; the crew at Hope 103.2 FM; the *Manly Daily*; the *Sydney Morning Herald*; and of course, my mates on the Grill Team at Triple M—the people who started this wild ride by passing my request on to Hugh Jackman to play a part in Rachel's birthday video.

Carolyn Coulton, who guided me through the minefield with grace and outstanding professionalism; and Russell Crowe, for words whispered in my ear late one night before Christmas. When Maximus speaks, you listen.

Oprah, who, by taking the time to care about us, gave me a platform to stand on whereby I could be taken seriously by the decision makers of our nation.

And all of you who support me here with letters of kindness and encouragement. Not a day goes by that I don't look up and see the outstretched arm of a stranger, lifting me out of the mud with the kindest of words, the most compassionate of hearts. All of you who added your own voice to mine, thank you.

And to heaven, to my God, who has brought me here for such a time as this, for reasons I cannot possibly begin to understand: be it unto me according to Your will.

I know what it means to say those words, and I am not afraid.

YO-YO

We've been on holiday in the United States for the past three weeks. It's the first time in twenty months that I've had a break from treatment, and it has been a chance to start to feel normal again and recharge the batteries. My skin has just now started to get back to its pre-Erbitux self. Only mild itching and burning, and the bleeding has stopped pretty much completely.

Visiting friends
Tony and Brenda
in Minnesota

I had blood work taken yesterday, and I got my results back just a few minutes ago.

It isn't good.

My markers have tripled while we were away, and all are now out of safe zones, including liver enzymes. This makes the third time I've had them come down only to go back up and have to start all over again. I have a meeting with my oncologist on Friday, and I'm guessing he will order more CT scans to determine whether or not the increase in my markers is due to the cancer spreading elsewhere or just due to activity in the liver. Either way, it's probably going to mean more chemo, a liver resection, or more radiation—or all three. More chemo means more Erbitux, and back to mutant status. More burning, more itching, and more bleeding. It also means there's no way they will consider reversing my stoma for the time being. Sigh.

I don't really have any more to add right now. I was driving along pretty happily, but it appears I have run over some nails on the road, and all the air has gone out of my tires.

I'll let you know more when I do.

Please pray.

DEAD MAN WALKING

I'm not being melodramatic. Not being melancholic. It's just the reality of my situation.

Unless God intervenes, I will die. There's a time bomb in my liver, and I need to know which wire to cut. The clock is ticking.

Some people have remarked on one of my previous comments, "I know what it means to say those words, and I am not afraid." They thought perhaps I meant that I was not afraid to die. That's not the case. I've already made known my fears with regard to this matter. They haven't changed. I'm human, and I'd very much like to continue to be human. But unless things start to change for the better, I am facing the very real prospect of death. But that's not what I meant when I wrote it.

I'm not afraid, but not because I am comfortable with the thought of dying—not at all. What I meant was that I am not afraid because I know I can trust God with my very life, because I know that He will deal with me lovingly and with great care.

How do I know this?

Matthew 10:29–31 (MSG) states:

"What's the price of a pet canary? Some loose change, right? And God cares what happens to it even more than you do. He pays even greater attention to you, down to the last detail—even numbering the hairs on your head!"

God cares about a tiny bird. He knows when one falls from the sky. That sounds like a loving nature to me—that He would care for something so small, and then care for me so much more.

If God is Love (1 John 4:8), then I can deduce that God is kind and protects (1 Corinthians 13:4).

From there I can see that God Himself wants to protect me and is there, ready to help. So while cancer is creeping around inside my body, busting to take me out and with one purpose in mind—to kill me—I still have the God of heaven on my side and He promises to help me. Not only that, but it reads in Psalm 91:11 (MSG):

> *He ordered his angels*
> *to guard you wherever you go.*
> *If you stumble, they'll catch you;*
> *their job is to keep you from falling.*

So I have God *and* angel armies looking out for me.

If I believe this God and say, "I follow Christ," then I must believe what He says. And because He is the way and *the truth* and the life (John 14:6), His words cannot be false. He cannot lie, because a lie cannot exist inside the truth. And I can be sure He will do what He says, because it reads in Numbers 23:19 (MSG):

> *God is not man, one given to lies,*
> *and not a son of man changing his mind.*
> *Does he speak and not do what he says?*
> *Does he promise and not come through?*

So as I lie here beside my boys in their beds, listening to the sound of their soft breathing, smelling the sweet scent of their skin, and watching their little chests rise and fall with each breath, I empty myself before God.

I now understand the concept of losing my life to find it (Matthew 10:39).

I came from dust, and to dust I will return. I'm nothing but dust without the breath of God, so once again I offer up to heaven the only words I know:

God, help.

You said You would. I'm here, waiting.

LAST/FIRST/LAST

I want to do something great with my life.

Some people would very generously suggest that perhaps I already have. Fighting cancer, Rachel's video, *Oprah*, lobbying the government—lots of things that might shoehorn me into that category. But truth be told, though I appreciate the kindness of their words, I don't consider my deeds thus far *great*. I don't say that out of some false sense of humility or modesty. I say it because I see myself as barely hanging on— "on the edge of a thread," as a friend of mine wrote in one of his songs.

The problem is, greatness takes time, and time is something I may or may not have.

When I say *great*, I don't mean I want to be someone that everybody considers wonderful or someone that everyone likes, because pursuing the approval and acclaim of others is, in my opinion, the fastest way to nowhere. The Bible even warns of such "greatness" in Luke 6:26 (CEV):

You are in for trouble when everyone says good things about you.

Fame and celebrity are fickle masters, and ambition— well, I know a lot of ambitious people, and I don't like them very much. Ambitious people often don't care who they tread on while climbing the ladder. It's only on the way down, when they're the ones being stepped on, that a realization of the impact of their own behavior sets in. But the damage is already done by then.

But back to greatness.

I'm happy to live a quiet life. In fact, I'm happy just to live a life, period. Rich, poor, success, failure, struggle, easy street, or any combination of the above. Just to live would be pretty sweet in my book. To live without physical pain and sickness—even better. But I'll take it, whichever way it comes. I have three very precious people depending on me. I don't intend to let them down.

When I was first diagnosed, once the sting from that initial slap had died down, I started taking stock of my life. Those first few weeks before I started chemotherapy, before I knew if I had a chance, before I knew if my body would respond to the chemical onslaught, I began to consider what might be said of me should my end be sooner rather than later. If my life was a shout from a cliff top somewhere, what would the echo sound like?

In the movie *Eddie and the Cruisers*, Eddie Wilson said, "What I want is songs that echo. The stuff we're doing now is like somebody's bedsheets. Spread 'em out, soil 'em, ship 'em out to laundry, you know? But our songs ... I want to be able to fold ourselves up in them forever."

I like that concept, even if it is from the lips of a movie character.

I want my life to be a life that, when it's over and done, is one that leaves behind memories and feelings that my loved ones can wrap themselves up in, find warmth in, find comfort in.

But how does one achieve this "greatness"?

In Mark 9:33–35 it reads:

> *They came to Capernaum. When he was in the house, [Jesus] asked them, "What were you arguing about on the road?" But they kept quiet because on the way they had argued about who was the greatest.*
>
> *Sitting down, Jesus called the Twelve and said, "Anyone who wants to be first must be the very last, and the servant of all."*

I'll tell you a story.

While we were away on holiday in the United States recently, we spent a lot of time in the hands of the Disney Company. Disneyland, Disney World, Disney hotels, even a Disney cruise. It was fantastic. Oprah said to us that life was all about energy and that we only have so much to go around; she was right. My batteries needed recharging, badly. So off we went.

At the end of our three-week trip, we found ourselves back in Los Angeles for a short time, not long enough to see good friends, but long enough to hit up Disneyland one last time before we left. We had been told we had to try to get a table at The Blue Bayou restaurant, which is part of the Pirates of the Caribbean ride. (Best ride there, next to the Star Tours journey through the *Star Wars* universe, in my opinion.) So we made a reservation, headed off to Tom Sawyer Island, and went looking for pirate treasure.

Our reservation time rolled around, and we found ourselves seated by the water. It was amazing. Lit only by lanterns and candles, the setting made it feel like we were in an authentic New Orleans/Louisiana bayou, complete with a jazz guitarist playing sad songs on what looked like a Gibson ES-335 semi-acoustic up on the balcony. Our waiter came over and introduced himself. He was a big black dude named Al. I liked him right away. Something Disney has done right is its employees. Our entire trip we were blown away by how nice and how helpful they were. You can have the biggest brand in the world, but if the day-to-day people on the floor are jerks, it's not going to last long. But Disney staff — 100 percent of the time in our experience — are the best advertising Disney has.

Enjoying our Disney cruise, July 2011

So back to Al. He took our order, and Rachel quickly went off to Splash Mountain. Jakob was asleep in his stroller, and Cody and I were playing with his *Star Wars* action figures on the table. After he took our order, Al and I got talking about where we were from, how we ended up here, and a little about my situation. By the end of the conversation I said to Al, "If you have a wife and kids, don't worry about 'the stuff.' Don't worry about what you feel you need to buy them or give them. Because one day, if you have to go, they're not going to remember 'the stuff'; they're going to remember you." I have no idea where it came from; it just happened. Al stood there for a minute in silence, turned to leave, turned back, turned to leave again, turned back, then finally said he was going to check on our order.

When Al came back, he approached in a very different manner. He came slowly and deliberately and said that he had done some checking and that "everything was taken care of." I asked him what that meant, and he told me that our meal was free—he was going to pay for it. I told him it was an incredibly generous gesture, but I couldn't let him do that. By the time drinks and sides were added, it was nearly $100, maybe more. But he wouldn't hear of it. I tried again, but he said it was something he really wanted to do, and off he went.

I sat there, very thankful the room was quite dark, because I was so moved by what Al had done I had tears rolling down my cheeks. Rachel came back, soaked, and we had our meal. I didn't say much. I couldn't.

When it was time to go, I looked for Al. He came over, and I stood up and just hugged him. I told him how much it meant to us, his generosity and selflessness. I told him that maybe he didn't realize it, but what he thought he did in secret was actually witnessed by my Father in heaven.

In Matthew 25:40 it reads:

The King will reply, "Truly, whatever you did for one of the least of these brothers and sisters of mine, you did for me."

I told him that, seeing as how he wouldn't let me pay, all I could offer him was to ask that God look after him and his family. I knew He would, because He's been looking after me and mine. I put my right hand on his shoulder and said, "Jesus, bless this man." And there it was, the warm blanket over my shoulders. God was there. We hugged again, both of us with tears quietly running down our faces; we exchanged contact details, and our family went on our way to get ready for our flight.

Do you think Al woke up that day and decided he was going to do something great? I doubt it. He was probably just thinking it was going to be another day at work. I thought it was going to be a fun day at Disneyland, but I left being so deeply moved by one man's generosity and care. His greatness. What Al did for us will echo in my heart for as long as I live.

I think that's how you become truly great. You help others. You put yourself last so they can go first. You don't have to have a million dollars in the bank. What is it you have in your hand? What are you good at?

Are you a mechanic? Does someone you know need help with their car?

Are you a gardener? Is someone you know unable to tend their garden?

Are you an accountant? Does someone you know need help with their tax return?

Are you a stay-at-home mum who cooks a mean pasta? Do you know someone who could really do with some help at mealtime?

Are you a cleaner? Do you know someone who needs their house cleaned every now and then?

Are you a regular dude who sees a family in a restaurant and you want to pay their bill?

Do it. These are the sorts of things that make you great. These are the things that change the lives of others. I speak from experience. I know. All of the things listed above are things people have done and continue to do for my family and me.

Jesus said, "Whatever you do for one of the least of these, you do for me."

Love is a verb, a doing word.

Have a think about it. Then look around. Find someone who needs a hand.

We all do.

ONE DAY

This is why I do it.

Cody, Jakob: Daddy thinks the world of you both. One day you'll understand it all.

This is a video Kristian made of the boys.

zph.com/dlt/qr5

BECAUSE I CHOOSE TO

Agent Smith: Why, Mr. Anderson? Why do you do it? Why get up? Why keep fighting?

Do you believe you're fighting for something? For more than your survival?

Can you tell me what it is? Do you even know?

Is it freedom? Or truth? Perhaps peace?

Yes?

No?

Could it be for love?

Illusions, Mr. Anderson! Vagaries of perception. The temporary constructs of a feeble human intellect trying desperately to justify an existence that is without meaning or purpose. And all of them as artificial as the Matrix itself, although only a human mind could invent something as insipid as love. You must be able to see it, Mr. Anderson. You must know it by now. You can't win. It's pointless to keep fighting.

Why, Mr. Anderson? Why? Why do you persist?

Neo: Because I choose to.

THE MATRIX REVOLUTIONS (2003)

PLEASE, SIR, CAN I HAVE SOME MORE?

It's been a crazy few weeks.

I've been in three countries, shot a music documentary with one of my favorite bands, made new friends, and had a whole bunch of medical tests.

It was Jakob's birthday this week too. He turned three. I was diagnosed when he was just one year old, so he's only ever really known Daddy to be "a bit sick." Seeing his face light up as he opened his presents reminded me why this fight is so important. You can do whatever you want to my body, to my mind, but you will not see me give up this fight. For the sake of my children, if nothing else.

My cancer markers have been climbing steadily since we came home from our holiday, that upward trend we so don't like to see, so a PET scan was ordered. My first since diagnosis. It doesn't get any more detailed than a PET scan, and I was happy to have it done so we could find out what was going on inside of me.

My biggest fear was that the cancer had jumped to another part of my body.

After an anxious weekend awaiting the results, it was determined that, thankfully, we're still only dealing with the liver tumors. There are four of them that showed up black on the scan, the black indicating blood flow and activity. Two are at the top of my liver, and two at the bottom. Basically, they're really misbehaving. There was also one small tumor that appears to have "dropped" from my liver to my psoas muscle, which is located in the pelvis. The doctors seem to think this will be easily eradicated by some targeted radiation, so it will be monitored.

And that's where I'm headed again: radiation, SIRT.

I was hoping it would still be an option, as I had heard it could be a once-only type of thing due to its potency, and I had a pretty hefty dose of it in November 2010. Thankfully, the team at St. Vincent's Hospital here in Sydney were (1) very happy to see me and (2) in agreement that it would be feasible and we should get it underway as soon as possible. I'm scheduled to go in next Thursday for the "workup procedure," which is where they do a test run to make sure the blood flow is all correct and not leaking anywhere outside of the liver. Then, if that's all OK, it's the real procedure a week later.

Driving home from the hospital after being given the green light was not without its emotional moments.

I know it's probably going to sound odd, but I was elated.

I had walked in that day not knowing if I was going to be able to have another shot, and within one hour, I was driving home knowing that not only was I going to get another chance but that the doctors believed the procedure could be very effective at knocking off these problem tumors. It was really quite overwhelming: *I have another chance.*

Another chance to fight.

Another chance to live.

Another chance to celebrate the birth of my children.

Another chance to see another Christmas.

Another chance to wake up in the morning and see my beautiful wife lying next to me.

Another chance to be reminded of the grace of God that covers me daily as I walk through this seemingly endless valley. The neon lights that are His promises to me, lighting up the darkness, showing me the way forward when all other light fails.

This is surely the hardest, most intense set of circumstances I have ever faced. It's been two years now of nonstop treatment, and I am weary. It's taking its toll on me and my family. It's war, make no mistake. But I am ready for it. I have been to this particular battlefield before. I know the lay of the land, and I have a strategy that is proven and effective. Smith and Anderson will face off here once again. I'll take a beating, but I know Smith is going to come off second best.

I was made for this.

Life is calling loudly to me. It's not the way I imagined my life would pan out, but I'm here, armored up and ready to roll.

Just you try to stop me.

FROM RACHEL

Kristian loved New Zealand; we talked about moving there when he got well. He'd find work so easily because he was skilled in so many areas. So we seriously looked at moving there as a family. It would have been in our long-term plans to go there.

But very quickly and suddenly, we had to shift the whole way we thought about the future. After we received the Oprah money, we talked about what we'd do once he was well. We discussed doing a Disney cruise, and Kristian wanted to throw a big party for all the people who had supported us and helped us along the way. There were so many things that he wanted to do.

One night we were talking about it, and he said, "Why don't we do the Disney cruise now? We don't know what the future's going to hold; we've got the money now; you've got school holidays. Why don't we look at doing it now?"

Kristian started making inquiries, and he planned the whole thing. He loved having projects that involved planning, and he was a producer till the end. Initially, we couldn't get on a cruise in the July holidays, so we thought maybe we would do it during the Christmas holidays, because I would have more time off.

And then one spot came up. Kristian got an email that read, "We've had a cancellation. Do you want it?" He booked it in straightaway, and then we planned the flights and prepared to go see Tony and Brenda, our neighbors who had moved back to the States. While we were in Florida, we had some days at Disney World, and it ended up being just the best holiday.

I'm so glad we did it then, because a few months later everything came crashing down again. We were planning to go to New Zealand for Christmas, but by October it became obvious that we couldn't plan that far ahead anymore; we just had to take it day by day.

7

How the Light Gets In

AT THE FOOT OF HEAVEN

September 21, 2011

In his poem "At the Foot of Heaven," Kevin Max Smith talks about angels around his bed and how some were there to comfort, others to fight.

When I was younger, I was fortunate enough to work on a lot of concerts. Rock shows, theater, church gigs, and stinky, smoky pubs. It's where I learned my craft. One show in particular was with a band named dc Talk at the now-derelict Perth Entertainment Centre. Kevin Smith was one of the singers in the band.

I just got the call from the hospital, and the test implant or "workup procedure" is confirmed for tomorrow. From 7:30 a.m. to around about 5:00 p.m. Sydney time, I will be under live X-ray, CT scanners, and gamma cameras as they track blood flow and a dummy "tracer" particle to see where it all goes and if my body's blood vessels are still wired the right way to withstand the SIRT.

As much as I need this treatment, it requires a strength I do not possess on my own. I'm pretty fragile right now, emotionally speaking.

I know what's coming tomorrow, and as much as I have said I will do anything to continue this fight, the thought of what lies ahead is daunting. I know the discomfort that's coming. I know that for three hours afterward, I am going to have to lie perfectly still in recovery so the puncture in my hepatic artery can heal. I know that about an hour before I am discharged, Rachel and the kids will begin their journey to the hospital in peak-hour traffic to pick me up. I know that when I see them, it's going to be a struggle to maintain my composure and not burst into tears. Tears of relief, tears of weariness. I know that Cody will probably remember the last time he was there with me and that I bought him and Jakob a "special chocolate cake" from the café.

I hope I have the presence of mind to remember to get him another one.

I'm afraid. I am.

What if my "wiring" has changed? What if the answer is "no, it's not safe"? The people administering this procedure have done it more than 450 times before. They know what they're talking about.

What if?

What if?

What if?

God, I know I said "be it unto me according to Your will," and I stand by that. I'm going to be walking those corridors again tomorrow, and I'm scared. All I'm asking is that You meet me there, the same way You did nearly a year ago.

In You there is no darkness, because You are light.

Scatter the darkness, God.

Bring light.

Bring life.

I'm aching for it.

SIRT 2.0

Everything today went perfectly according to plan.

The doctors were able to head off a couple of potential leakage issues (as I understand it, anyway) and are very happy with the way things went. The way it's all worked out is even better than last time, and we're expecting good results.

Strangely enough, I don't remember much of the procedure after the local anesthetic went in and I felt the first little creepings of the catheter into my groin. Perhaps it's the time between treatments or just the fact that I have developed a pretty high tolerance for pain and discomfort over the course of two years' worth of chemo, but it was nowhere near as bad as I remembered it. I mostly remember smiling as they discovered my body has apparently grown a second hepatic artery since last time. I will investigate this strange little phenomenon and find out exactly what it means, or even if I heard it correctly, but it sounded like everyone thought it was pretty cool.

One other good thing to come from today was that they found a few smaller tumors on the liver that the PET scan missed. So they're going to be targeting those as well. Nobody gets a free ride on my liver.

All in all, it was a good day—so many familiar faces, and all of us happy to see each other again, even though the circumstances are so serious. There was a real sense of old friends getting back together. It's also the first day in quite a while in which I haven't felt the compulsion to eat. I'm weaning myself off the Dexamethasone this week, and it appears to be helping on the food-intake side of things. It will be nice to get back to a nonballooning and more stable weight range.

I've been given permission to take a camera crew in next week to film proceedings. It may take me a while to edit it all together, but quite a few people have asked what the procedure is like, so I figure this will be a good way to show you what happens.

Thank you for the support, everyone. It means so much to us.

Talk soon.

RECOVERY

Tomorrow will be one week since the SIR-Spheres procedure. I knew I would need a certain amount of physical isolation for a few days, and seeing as how it's school holidays, we decided Rachel and the boys should go to stay with her parents in New Zealand. That way they're protected, and I don't have to move out of our house.

They're having a great time. It makes me very happy.

I'm sitting/lying at home while the side effects take over—the pain I remember from the first time, the fever, the chills, the sweating that makes me have to change clothes multiple times in the middle of the night. But more than anything, the pain. I have good pain meds, but still it pierces through. I feel the heat of the radiation on my skin. I feel bubbling, popping in my liver, and at times the exhaustion is so bad that I feel like someone has literally kicked my legs out from under me.

I have had to steady myself against a wall a number of times while making the twenty-foot walk from the lounge to my bed. It's frightening.

But the physical pain is nothing this time. What's really hurting is the not knowing again. The three-month wait until we know how successful it has all been. And what worries me is that the last time we suspended chemo while the radiation did its thing, which was a welcome break, the tumor in my bowel began to grow. And of course we remember what happened at Christmas.

But the most painful thing of all is walking past the boys' bedroom door and seeing their empty beds. Cody's with his dinosaur blankets, and Jakob's with Thomas the Tank Engine. I walk down the hall and there are photos of their beautiful little faces, smiling out at me. And there are new photos Rach is sending me from NZ, so right now I'm sitting here weeping so hard I can barely see. Sobbing so deep it feels like my stomach will explode, since all of this is because I love them so much. All of the treatment and everything else that comes with it is so I can stay alive for them.

GOD!

Save us!

Save our family. PLEASE! Save *me*.

Take this disease from my body and this pain from my heart, from all our hearts.

I don't know what else to say. God, please help, once and for all. My heart is breaking more and more every day. I don't know how much longer I can take this.

Rachel, Cody, and Jakob, I love you so much. I wish I could show you just how much.

NUMBERING MY DAYS

It has been a very hard few weeks. The SIRT recovery is continuing, but not without its own battles. The exhaustion is extreme, and the night sweats and fever are very unpleasant. But I'm getting there. I have been in the hospital for the past week with a case of pneumonia. Not an uncommon side effect of the SIRT, but enough to put me in a hospital bed for a week. While I was there, they found I had fluid in my stomach, which is why I have been bloated lately. It has been drained, but it indicates a possible significant deterioration in my condition. If my stomach fluid isn't draining, it means something is blocking the drains. In my case as a cancer patient, it usually means it's being blocked by cancer cells.

Which leads me to my updated prognosis.

On Saturday my oncologist sat down with Rachel and me and told us I have three to six months left to live. I'm not responding to any of the drugs available to me. To continue might bring minor results, but the painful side effects would far outweigh any curative benefit. Living life is one thing, but the quality of that life is important too.

It was awful. It was like we were right back at Diagnosis Day all over again. I was devastated, because it means all my hard work, all my fighting, has really been for nothing. We're nowhere near remission and certainly nowhere near a cure. Heartbreaking.

So Rachel and I spent a lot of time crying and hugging each other and telling each other how much we love the other. Both of us had our hearts shattered again.

So here it is now: my days are numbered. Unless God

intervenes and brings a miracle, I am going to die. Rachel will become a widow, and Cody and Jakob will have no father. I'm in the process now of writing a book for them with photos and letters, full of memories and anything I can pass on to them that may be of use as they continue living their lives. Tying up loose ends, financially making sure they are taken care of, etc. I have to do these things. To leave them undone would be irresponsible and unfair to Rachel. It's going to be hard enough as it is.

Please pray for us, as a family, for me as an individual. For healing, for the miracle.

I haven't stopped believing.

I never will.

Though he slay me, yet will I hope in him.

JOB 13:15

IN DEFENSE OF DADDY

The other night I was helping Rachel put the boys to bed, as we do, and I was cuddling up to Jakob in his bed. He loves to tell me all about his day and what he did. It's very cute. I began to test the waters with him and told him that Daddy will always live in his heart, no matter what happens. He looked at me and said, "In my heart? Oh. OK." Then we tested it a few times. "Where will Daddy live?"

Jakob: "Ummm ... kindy?"

Daddy: "Noooo ..."

Jakob: "In my heart?"

Daddy: "Yes, that's right. So even if I have to leave, I will always love you and live in your heart. Sometimes people have to go away and can't come back, like when they're very sick."

Cody walked in at that exact moment and got very angry. "NO!" he shouted. "YOU CAN'T LEAVE! Why are you going, and why can't you come back? There's only one daddy for a family, and you're our daddy ... and ... and ... you *can't* go!"

He had tears running down his cheeks, and the look on his face was pure fury. He was angry.

At that point I couldn't contain it anymore and collapsed in sobs. We talked it through a bit more, and then we prayed with them. Pretty soon they were asleep, but it wasn't easy.

Somehow I have to help my boys understand what's coming.

Dear God, no father should ever have to do this.

WOULD THE REAL REALITY PLEASE STAND UP?

It's been a while now since my prognosis was updated from "treatable" to "terminal."

We've prepared as much of our lives as possible for the (medically) inevitable. Our parents and friends have been a great help in getting this rolling, flying in from Perth and Auckland. Physically we've had to sort through three years' worth of stuff in storage—things we had stashed away in a storage unit because they wouldn't fit in our little house. Electronically it's been getting all our finances and authorizations sorted and flowing into the one right place. That's nearly done, except for a couple of small things. But otherwise we're on track.

I'm being visited every day by a home nursing service so that a nurse can drain my stomach port to bearable levels. They've also given me a wheelchair, which is very handy, as I can't walk without becoming breathless or exhausted after a few steps. My bowel is incredibly active and quite tender as a result, so that's been added to the pain-management schedule. Yes, I have a schedule for managing my pain. The first few weeks were trial and error, but now we seem to be settling on a preferred treatment style that the palliative oncologist is happy with. In his mind, pain management is key. "If you're not comfortable, then I'm failing," he says.

Anyway ... the drugs really alter my perception of reality. They also severely diminish my ability to use my body other than for standing up or lying down. I really hate it.

I feel so much less than human, but there's nothing I can do unless I want to leave this earth a bawling mass of pain. That doesn't really sit well with me either, so excuse me while I go back and put my zombie outfit on.

THE FINAL CALL

The following is Kristian's final blog, posted after his death. It was posted by Rachel after he had an inkling it was his time to go.

There is a crack in everything. That's how the light gets in.

As mentioned at the start of this journey, it's a Leonard Cohen lyric. The truth is, we're all broken, we're all cracked, and what so many people see as a fault or a malfunction really is something to be considered useful. I'm not sure how much longer I have left, but it appears that the physical and medical signs are all pointing to my end.

And what a great time to go, right at Christmastime. Just wonderful.

The time my Savior was brought into the world is the very same time He decides to call me home. The irony is astounding.

While I struggle to find any logical rhyme or reason in all of this, my commitment to following Him has not changed. People look at me like I'm crazy. How can I trust God to deliver me from this madness when this madness means losing my wife and two beautiful children? And the answer is, I simply don't know.

It's the light that permeates the brokenness. It's the light that the three wise men followed that night when Christ was born. It's the light that just came to be when God said "Let there be light" on the first day of creation. It's unexplainable. And as I said before, even though it makes no sense, I will follow it until my very end.

It's the light that shines for every man and woman, and thankfully it shines for me, lest I be lost in the darkness that surrounds me without it.

Thank you for journeying with me this far. I pray you find the same peace I have.

Kristian checking his final blog post, December 29, 2011

FROM RACHEL

We didn't know if Kristian would make Christmas, particularly after the scares we had in November. I wasn't even sure he was going to make Cody's birthday on November 22, because by that point he'd had enough. He was ready to go. Unless we got our eleventh-hour miracle, he knew that this was probably it, and he was sick of waiting around and feeling sick.

He just never bounced back from his last radiation treatment, never got his energy back. I often wonder if he hadn't had that last radiation treatment in September, whether he might have felt better and lasted longer. It really knocked him around, and that's when he got the pneumonia and ended up in the hospital. Then we found he had fluid in his stomach, and that was the start of a really quick downward spiral.

Kristian had all these things he wanted to do, and he started realizing they were not going to happen. He began the process of deregistering his business, and he sold his other iTunes business. He started getting a document ready for me with all the bank details and showed me how to do all these things that I didn't know how to do.

From November on it was a real roller coaster. Kristian was so incapacitated by that point. He was sleeping twenty-two hours a day, and when he was awake, he couldn't move his legs because they were so swollen. Every four or five days, he'd have an episode where he was completely overwhelmed and depressed and feeling so sick that he was praying, "God, take me. Just take me, please." At the same time I'd be praying, "Don't take him. I'm not ready. Don't take him."

I remember one day my friends Michelle and Heidi came over

to the house to pray with Kristian. We went into the bedroom to see him and to pray with him, and all of a sudden he just got overwhelmed. He was sobbing, and he looked at me and said, "I'm ready to go. I'm ready to go."

Heidi and I made eye contact, and I was thinking, "Crap, it's going to happen now. I'm not ready. I took the boys to kindy this morning and they said good-bye to Daddy, but it was just a little good-bye." Heidi started to read the Bible out loud to bring Kristian peace, and Michelle was praying, and I was lying next to Kristian on the bed watching his chest rise and fall, thinking he's just going to go.

For about an hour that's how it was, and it was awful. Then all of a sudden Kristian sat up and said, "Oh, I remember such-and-such owes us three grand for that work." So I reassured him, "You don't have to worry about that."

Obviously his brain was ticking over because ten minutes later he sat up and said, "And such-and-such owes us some money for those tapes. Make sure you write that down." And then, after about another fifteen minutes, he sat back up again: "Rach, I'm really hungry. Have we got anything to eat?"

Clearly that wasn't going to be the day that Kristian died.

But gradually those episodes started occurring more often. During the last couple of weeks in the hospital, it was a couple of times a day. He'd look at me and say, "Rach, I want to go. I want to go." And I'd say to him, "I know. Just let go when you're ready." But it seemed he was still here for a reason. The doctors said that his heart was still beating well, his pulse was strong, he was warm, he was still eating — physically it seemed he could go on for months. He just didn't want to be here.

I think he did eventually decide it was time to go. It was his ordained time, and there was nothing we could do about that, as much as I would have loved for him to stay.

During the last weeks, I slept on a hospital bed next to him. Every morning he'd roll over, and I'd be stoked that he was still here. But he'd look at me and say, "I'm still here," and he would sound so crushed. I was utterly devastated, but I think he was clinically depressed on top of everything else. He was just desperate to be in heaven. He knew that then it would all be over; in his mind, it would be a blink of an eye and he would be there. For him it was the better option, and I knew that, but I still didn't want him to go.

The doctors and nurses had said there was a piece of tumor that might break off and get lodged in one of his arteries, and it could be over all of a sudden, or he might gently slip away in his sleep. So when he didn't wake up this particular morning, I knew it wouldn't be far off.

The oncology nurses had explained to me that the deeper into an unconscious state the patient goes, the lower their oxygen saturation is. Things are just slowly but gently shutting down, and that's how he went: he just faded out.

Kristian went to heaven on January 2, 2012, just after 8:00 a.m., at Manly Hospital. His passing was truly peaceful, and he had a tear in his eye as he left, and I have no doubt that he was looking at the face of Jesus.

I miss him every day.

Rachel's Eulogy for Kristian

There is a crack in everything. That's how the light gets in ... The truth is, we're all broken, we're all cracked, and what so many people see as a fault or a malfunction really is something to be considered useful.

FROM KRISTIAN'S FINAL BLOG POST

My husband never tried to be anything he wasn't, and he didn't apologize for that. His only desire was that through his weaknesses, more of God would be revealed. He was opinionated, black and white, and at times brutally honest — but it was always in the desire for perfection, which was evidenced in the projects he created and worked on.

Kristian used to mix the sound at church, and often, when I was singing, he would point to me and tell me I was singing flat. I didn't get any special treatment just because I was his wife. If I wasn't up to scratch and was ruining his mix, he'd mute me without hesitation, as he did many other singers.

Yet whenever we had disagreements at home, he was always the first to come to me and apologize, to put things right.

He was also the most passionate, romantic, impulsive, generous, and brave man I have ever known. I have lost count of the times a huge box from Roses Only would turn up at school for me, filled with a dozen or more long-stemmed red roses—just because. He bought this dress I'm wearing today in LA on his trip to Corey and Aimee's wedding, because he saw it in a window and knew that I would like it. He bought me diamonds on more than one occasion and surprised me one night with a limo ride into the city to a fancy restaurant for a degustation dinner, just because we had a babysitter and he wanted to spoil me. And of course he made me a pretty special DVD for my birthday not that long ago.

Kristian was exceptionally brave, not just through this cancer journey. Before we had children, we were driving somewhere and witnessed quite a serious collision between a small truck and a larger one. The smaller truck was flipped onto its side. Kristian leaped out of our car and grabbed a few other guys, and together they righted the small truck so the terrified driver could get out. Another time, Kristian was taking Cody to the mall for ice cream; on the way he drove past a woman screaming as her golden retriever was being attacked by a Staffordshire terrier. Without thinking about his own safety, Kristian pulled the car over, leaped out, and proceeded to try to separate the two dogs.

He was a dedicated and devoted father who adored his two boys. Knowing he wouldn't see them grow up was what tore up his heart the most. I see so much of him in them, though. From Cody's stubbornness and how he sees things so black and white, to Jakob's persistence, their daddy is always going to be in them and a part of them.

Before I go any farther, I want to make special mention of the incredible staff at Manly Hospital, firstly in the oncology ward. Dr. Page, Dr. Copeman, Trisha, and Tania became some of Kristian's favorite people in the whole world, and he knew they were going to bat for him every day. Thank you so much for everything. Thank you, too, to the wonderful nurses from South Wing Four, who made his last days so comfortable and gave me such peace that he was being cared for when I couldn't be there.

We have received so much love from so many people that I can't mention everyone, but thank you especially to our wonderful pastors here at church who have helped to carry us for the last two years. Without you, I would be curled up in a little ball right now.

This two-year cancer battle has been exactly that—a battle. It's been a battle for Kristian not only physically but also emotionally. The effort it took him to get out of bed some mornings was not because of the physical pain he felt, but the emotional pain.

Fighting to get Erbitux onto the PBS was a reason he found to get out of bed when he didn't feel well. Seeing the fruit of his labor was so rewarding, and knowing that he had helped so many people made the burden he carried just that little bit lighter. We were so blessed to have the opportunity to meet Oprah and to have the funds given to us from Microsoft through her, because it allowed us to have the holiday together that we'd planned to do once Kristian had beaten his cancer. The memories that we made on the holiday were amazing, and I know that God had His hand on it in so many ways.

The last three months that Kristian and the boys and I had together were so precious. He was so desperate to be rid of his body and to be out of his torment, living it up with the angels. I was so grateful for every morning that I woke to have him wake up beside me. I treasured the evenings we had, when I would wash him and change his sheets, getting him comfortable for the night. On the night of December 30, I said good night to him as I did every night, but the following morning he didn't wake up. Two mornings later, he slipped quietly into eternity. I know he saw Jesus in those last moments. I know he was finally receiving his crown from the King of kings, and I know he heard, "Well done, good and faithful servant."

We spent a number of evenings in the last three months watching the Lord of the Rings trilogy. We'd watched it many times before, but the last time was particularly poignant. In the final scene of *The Fellowship of the Ring*, Frodo is preparing to go off on his own, and he says, "I wish the ring had never come to me. I wish none of this had happened." Gandalf replies, "So do all who live to see such times. But that is not for them to decide. All we have to decide is what to do with the time that is given us." Many nights during the cancer battle, we would be lying in bed together, and typically I would be the one crying, telling him that I didn't want him to go, and he would be comforting me. We would together try to figure out a reason for all of this, why our family had to go through this and what God was going to accomplish through it all. Jeremiah 29:11 says, "'For I know the plans I have for you,' declares the LORD, 'plans to prosper you and not to harm you, plans to give you hope and a future.'" We realized that the reason we had to bear this burden was because of all of you. We already had our hope and our future in Jesus. We often wondered how people could go through something as awful as this without the assurance that God has got it all under control and knowing that there is something better coming afterward.

After Kristian had died, I helped a beautiful nurse named Lauren wash his body, and it broke my heart to see again how wretched his earthly body was. He was covered in scars. He was skin and bone in some places, but bloated and swollen in others. He had a colostomy bag, a catheter, a portacath, an ascites stomach drain, and a butterfly intravenous needle all hanging off him. But it made me realize once again that our time here is fleeting. It is but a fraction of the eternity that God has planned for us. We are frail, fragile, and breakable.

It is not a coincidence that you have made contact with Kristian. I don't believe there are any coincidences in this life. Everything happens because God has preordained it, and there is a purpose. The fact that you are sitting here in church—some of you for the first time ever or, at the very least, the first time in a long while—is no coincidence. God has had His finger on your life since before you were born, leading you to this moment. You did not just "stumble" onto Kristian's blog. You did not randomly make contact with him through Facebook, Twitter, work, or through friends. His very existence here on earth was, we believe, to bring you to a place where you need to question what it is you put your faith in, what it is that you hold important.

Life is short. Even if you lived to be a hundred years old, that is but a blink in eternity. I want you all to know, just as Kristian did, that there is something better for you after this lifetime. And I know that Kristian would love to see you all again. God bless you.

Kristian's celebration video

zph.com/dlt/qr6

Thank You

To the people who have partnered with us through this journey and have made this book possible, I want to say thank you. Thank you for all the meals you've cooked, washing you've done, bills you've paid, cleaning, minding our children, and shoulders to cry on.

Rachel Anderson

Acknowledgments

FOREWORD

"Anthem" by Leonard Cohen. Composed by Leonard Cohen. Courtesy of Sony/ATV Music Publishing.

CHAPTER 1: LET ME BRING YOU UP TO SPEED

"Blood Brothers" by Bruce Springsteen. Copyright © 1996 Bruce Springsteen (ASCAP). Reprinted by permission. International copyright secured. All rights reserved.

CHAPTER 2: GOING THE DISTANCE

"Better Way" by Mumsdollar. Copyright © 2010 Mumsdollar. Reprinted by permission.

"Hallelujah" by Leonard Cohen. Composed by Leonard Cohen. Courtesy of Sony/ATV Music Publishing.

Lyrics from "Wind in His Hair/Can You Go the Distance" by Chris Falson © 1992 Leather Chair Songs — c/o Sounds Dangerous LLC, PO Box 1147, Studio City, CA 91614, USA

CHAPTER 3: ONE OF THE LUCKY PEOPLE

"The Man with the Nail Scars" (Meece/Liles/Hudson) © Meece Music/World Music LLC/Ariose Music. Meece Music

& World Music licensed courtesy of CopyCare Pacific Pty Ltd. [Also courtesy of Crossroad Publishing.]

CHAPTER 4: WONDERFUL INCONVENIENCE

"If It Be Your Will" by Leonard Cohen. Composed by Leonard Cohen. Courtesy of Sony/ATV Music Publishing.

"When All Around Has Fallen" by Delirious? Composed by Martin James Smith. Courtesy of Crossroad Publishing.

CHAPTER 5: CALLING ALL ANGELS

December 14, 2010: Sydney, NSW. United States talk show host Oprah Winfrey, with cancer patient Kristian Anderson and his wife, Rachel Anderson, during the taping of *The Oprah Winfrey Show* at the Sydney Opera House. Published: *The Daily Telegraph*—December 15, 2010. Photo: John Grainger © Newspix / News Ltd / 3rd Party Managed Reproduction & Supply Rights

CHAPTER 6: DEAD MAN WALKING

"I Will Not Lay Down" by Margaret Becker. Composed by T. Bieck/T. Leah. Courtesy of Crossroad Publishing.

Loving husband and father, and inspiration to thousands, **Kristian Anderson** was also a music producer, sound engineer, lighting technician, and film editor. Born in Sydney, he and his family moved to Perth when he was a child. There, he worked as a film editor at Editel and Channel 9 before moving back to Sydney, where he studied music at the C3 Church School of Creative Arts and worked as a freelance editor. He worked at Frame, Set & Match in Sydney for five years and then at RASH TV in Narrabeen before setting up his own company, Musikwerks.

Although Kristian once prayed that he would marry neither a New Zealander nor a singer, his wife-to-be had both of these qualifications. Kristian and **Rachel Anderson** married in 2003 and had two boys, Cody and Jakob. Rachel teaches science at Oxford Falls Grammar School in Sydney.

Share Your Thoughts

With the Author: Your comments will be forwarded to the author when you send them to *zauthor@zondervan.com*.

With Zondervan: Submit your review of this book by writing to *zreview@zondervan.com*.

Free Online Resources at
www.zondervan.com

Zondervan AuthorTracker: Be notified whenever your favorite authors publish new books, go on tour, or post an update about what's happening in their lives at www.zondervan.com/authortracker.

Daily Bible Verses and Devotions: Enrich your life with daily Bible verses or devotions that help you start every morning focused on God. Visit www.zondervan.com/newsletters.

Free Email Publications: Sign up for newsletters on Christian living, academic resources, church ministry, fiction, children's resources, and more. Visit www.zondervan.com/newsletters.

Zondervan Bible Search: Find and compare Bible passages in a variety of translations at www.zondervanbiblesearch.com.

Other Benefits: Register to receive online benefits like coupons and special offers, or to participate in research.

ZONDERVAN®